BHAKTI YOGA

SWAMI VIVEKANANDA

SANAGE
PUBLISHING HOUSE

Paperback: 978-939156010-2

Printed by: Manipal Technologies Limited, Manipal

Sanage Publishing House LLP
Mumbai, India

sanagepublishing@gmail.com

That which exists is One: sages call it variously.

Rigveda, I, 164, 46.

CONTENTS

BHAKTI-YOGA

PARÂ-BHAKTI-YOGA

BHAKTI-YOGA

EPIGRAPH

"He is the Soul of the Universe; He is immortal; His is the Rulership; He is the All-Knowing, the All-Pervading, the Protector of the Universe, the Eternal Ruler. None else is there efficient to govern the World eternally. He who at the beginning of creation projected *Brahmâ* (I. e., the universal consciousness), and Who delivered the Vedas unto him seeking liberation I go for refuge unto that Effulgent One Whose light turns the understanding towards the *Âtman*."

Śwetâsvatara Upanîshad, VI. 17–18.

I. Definition Of Bhakti

Bhakti-yoga is a genuine, real search after the Lord, a search beginning, continuing and ending in Love. One single moment of the madness of extreme love to God brings us eternal freedom. *"Bhakti,"* says Nârada in his explanation of the *Bhakti Aphorisms,* "is intense love to God." "When a man gets it, he loves all, hates none; he becomes satisfied for ever." "This love cannot be reduced to any earthly benefit," because as long as worldly desires last that kind of love does not come. *"Bhakti* is greater than *Karma*, greater than *Yoga*, because these are intended for an object in view, while *Bhakti* is its own fruition, its own means and its own end."

Bhakti has been the one constant theme of our sages. Apart from the special writers on *Bhakti*, such as Sândilya or Nârada, the great commentators on the *Vyâsa-Sûtras,* evidently advocates of Knowledge (*Jnâna*), have also something very suggestive to say about Love. Even when the commentator is anxious to explain many, if not all, of the texts so as to make them import a sort of dry knowledge, the *sûtras*, in the chapter on worship especially, do not lend themselves to be easily manipulated in that fashion.

There is not really so much difference between Knowledge (*Jnâna*) and Love (*Bhakti*) as people sometimes imagine.

We shall see as we go on that in the end they converge and meet at the same point. So also, it is with *Râja-yoga,* which, when pursued as a means to attain liberation, and not (as unfortunately it frequently becomes in the hands of charlatans and mystery-mongers) as an instrument to hoodwink the unwary, leads us also to the same goal.

The one great advantage of *Bhakti* is that it is the easiest, and the most natural way to reach the great divine end in view; its great disadvantage is that in its lower forms it oftentimes degenerates into hideous fanaticism. The fanatical crew in Hinduism, or Mahomedanism, or Christianity, have always been almost exclusively recruited from these worshippers on the lower planes of *Bhakti*. That singleness of attachment (*Nishtha*) to a loved object, without which no genuine love can grow, is very often also the cause of the denunciation of everything else. All the weak and undeveloped minds in any religion or country have only one way of loving their own ideal, i. *e.*, by hating every other ideal. Herein is the explanation of why the same man who is so lovingly attached to his own ideal of God, so devoted to his own ideal of religion, becomes a howling fanatic as soon as he sees or hears anything of any other ideal. This kind of love is somewhat like the canine instinct of guarding the master's property from intrusion; only even the dog's instinct is better than the reason of man, for the dog never mistakes its master for an enemy in whatever dress he may come before it. Again, the fanatic loses all power of judgment. Personal considerations are in his case of such absorbing interest that to him it is no question at all what a man says whether it is right or wrong; but the one thing he is always particularly careful to know is, who says it. The same man who is kind, good, honest, and loving, to people of his own opinion will not hesitate to do the vilest deeds, when they are directed against persons beyond the pale of his own religious brotherhood.

But this danger exists only in that stage of *Bhakti* which is called the *preparatory* (gauni). When *Bhakti* has become ripe and has passed into that form which is called *the supreme* (para) no more is there any fear of these hideous manifestations of fanaticism; that soul which is overpowered by this higher form of *Bhakti* is too near the God of Love to become an instrument for the diffusion of hatred.

It is not given to all of us to be harmonious in the building up of our characters in this life: yet we know that that character is of the noblest type in which all these three knowledge and love and *yoga* are harmoniously fused. Three things are necessary for a bird to fly the two wings and the tail as a rudder for steering. *Jnâna* (knowledge) is the one wing, *Bhakti* (love) is the other, and *Yoga* is the tail that keeps up the balance. For those who cannot pursue all these three forms of worship together in harmony, and take up, therefore, *Bhakti* alone as their way, it is necessary always to remember that forms and ceremonials, though absolutely necessary for the progressive soul, have no other value than taking us on to that state in which we feel the most intense love to God.

There is a little difference in opinion between the teachers of Knowledge and those of Love, though both admit the power of *Bhakti*. The *Jnânins* hold *Bhakti* to be an instrument of liberation, the *Bhaktas* look upon it both as the instrument and the thing to be attained. To my mind this is a distinction without much difference. In fact, *Bhakti*, when used as an instrument, really means a lower form of worship, and the higher form becomes inseparable from the lower form of realisation at a later stage. Each seems to lay a great stress upon his own peculiar method of worship, forgetting that with perfect love true knowledge is bound to come even unsought, and that from perfect knowledge true love is inseparable.

Bearing this in mind let us try to understand what the great

Vedântic commentators have to say on the subject. In explaining the Sûtra *Âvrittirasakridupadeśât* Bhagavân Śankara says:

"Thus, people say, 'He is devoted to the king, He is devoted to the Guru; they say this of him who follows his Guru, and does so, having that following as the one end in view.' Similarly, they say 'The loving wife meditates on her loving husband;' here also a kind of eager and continuous remembrance is meant." This is devotion according to Śankara.

"Meditation again is a constant remembrance (of the thing meditated upon) flowing like an unbroken stream of oil poured out from one vessel to another. When this kind of remembering has been attained (in relation to God) all bondages breaks. Thus, it is spoken of in the scriptures regarding constant remembering as a means to liberation. This remembering again is of the same form as seeing, because it is of the same meaning, as in the passage, 'When He who is far and near is seen the bonds of the heart are broken, all doubts vanish, and all effects of work disappear.' (He who is near can be seen, but he who is far can only be remembered. Nevertheless, the scripture says that we have to see Him who is near as well as Him who is far, thereby indicating to us that the above kind of *remembering* is as good as seeing.) "This remembrance when exalted assumes the same form as seeing......Worship is constant remembering as may be seen from the essential texts of scriptures. Knowing, which is the same as repeated worship, has been described as constant remembering. ......Thus, the memory, which has attained to the height of what is as good as direct perception, is spoken of in the *Śruti* as a means of liberation. 'This *Âtman* is not to be reached through various sciences, nor by intellect, nor by much study of the Vedas. Whomsoever this *Âtman* desires by him is the Atman attained, unto him this *Âtman* discovers himself.' Here after saying that mere hearing, thinking, and meditating are not the means of attaining this *Âtman*, it is said, 'Whom this *Âtman* desires by him the *Âtman* is attained.' The extremely beloved is desired; by whomsoever this *Âtman* is extremely beloved, he becomes the most beloved of the *Âtman*. So that this beloved may attain the *Âtman*, the Lord himself helps. For it has been said by the Lord: 'Those who are constantly attached to me and worship me with love I give that direction to their will by which they come to me.' Therefore, it is said that, to whomsoever this remembering, which is of the same form as direct perception, is very dear, because it is dear to the Object of such memory-perception, he is desired by the Supreme *Âtman*, by him the Supreme *Âtman* is attained. This constant remembrance is denoted by the word *Bhakti*."

So, says *Bhagavân Râmânuja* in his commentary on the *Sûtra* Athâto Brahma Jijnâsâ.

In commenting on the *Sûtra* of Patanjali *Îśvara Pranidhânâdvâ* i. e., 'By the worship of the Supreme Lord,' Bhoja says, "*Pranidhânâ* is that sort of *Bhakti* in which, without seeking results, such as sense-enjoyments, etc., all works are dedicated to that Teacher of teachers." Also, Bhagavân Vyâsa, when commenting on the same, defines *Pranidhânâ* as "the form of *Bhakti* by which the mercy of the Supreme Lord comes to the *yogin* and blesses him by granting him his desires." According to Śândilya, "*Bhakti* is intense Love to God." The best definition is, however, that given by the king of *Bhaktas*, Prahlâda: "That deathless love which the ignorant have for the fleeting objects of the senses as I keep meditating on Thee may not that (sort of intense) love (for Thee) slip away from my heart." *Love!* For whom? For the Supreme Lord *Îśvara*. Love for any other being, however great, cannot be *Bhakti*; for, as Râmânuja says in his *Śrî Bhâshya* quoting an ancient *Âchârya*, i. e., a great teacher. "From Brahmâ to a clump of grass all things that live in the world are slaves of birth and death caused by *Karma*; therefore, they cannot be helpful as objects of meditation, because they are all in ignorance and subject to change." In commenting on the word *anurakti* used by Śândilya, the commentator *Svapneśvara* says that it means *anu*, after, and *rakti*, attachment; *i. e.*, the attachment which comes after the knowledge of the nature and glory of God; else a blind attachment to anyone, *e. g.*, to wife or children would be *Bhakti*.

We plainly see, therefore, that *Bhakti* is a series or succession of mental efforts at religious realisation beginning with ordinary worship and ending in supremely intense love for the *Îśvara*.

II. The Philosophy Of Îśvara

Who is *Îśvara*? "From Whom is the birth, continuation and dissolution of the universe," He is *Îśvara* "the Eternal, the Pure, the Ever Free, the Almighty, the

All-Knowing, the All-Merciful, the Teacher of all teachers;" and above all "He, the Lord is, of His own nature, inexpressible Love."

These certainly are the definitions of a personal God. Are there then two Gods? The "Not this, Not this," the *Satchit-ânanda*, the Existence-Knowledge-Bliss, of the philosopher, and this God of Love of the *Bhakta*? No, it is the same *Satchit-ânanda* who is also the God of Love, the impersonal and personal in one. It has always to be understood that the personal God worshipped by the *Bhakta* is not separate or different from the *Brahman*. All is *Brahman*, the One without a second: only the *Brahman*, as unity or absolute, is too much of an abstraction to be loved and worshipped; so, the *Bhakta* chooses the relative aspect of *Brahman*, that is, *Îśvara*, the Supreme Ruler. To use a simile: *Brahman* is as the clay or substance out of which an infinite variety of articles are fashioned. As clay, they are all one; but form or manifestation differentiates them. Before ever one of them was made, they all existed potentially in the clay; and, of course, they are identical substantially; but when formed, and so long as the form remains, they are separate and different; the clay-mouse can never become a clay-elephant, because, as manifestations, form alone makes them what they are, though as unformed clay they are all one. *Îśvara* is the highest manifestation of the absolute reality, or, in other words, the highest possible reading of the Absolute by the human mind. Creation is eternal, and so also is *Îśvara*.

In the fourth *pâda* of the fourth chapter of his *Sûtras*, after stating the almost infinite power and knowledge which will come to the liberated soul after the attainment of *Moksha*, Vyasa makes the remark, in an aphorism, that none, however, will get the power of creating, ruling, and dissolving the universe, because that belongs to God alone. In explaining the Sutra, it is easy for the dualistic commentators to show how it is ever impossible for a subordinate soul, *Jîva*, to have the infinite power and total independence of God. The thorough dualistic commentator *Madhvâchârya* deals with this passage in his usual summary method by quoting a verse from the Varâha-Purâna.

In explaining this aphorism the commentator, *Râmânuja*, says: This doubt being raised, whether among the powers of the liberated souls is included that unique power of the Supreme One, that is, of creation, etc., of the universe and even the Lordship of all, or whether, without that, the glory of the liberated consists only in the direct perception of the Supreme One, we get as an argument the following: It is reasonable that the liberated get the Lordship of the universe, because the scriptures say, 'He attains extreme sameness with the Pure One,' because, as the scriptures say, he attains to extreme sameness with the Supreme One and all his desires are realized. Now extreme sameness and realization of all desires cannot be attained without the unique power of the Supreme Lord, namely that of governing the universe. Therefore, to attain the realization of all desires and the extreme sameness with the Supreme, we must all admit that the liberated get the power of ruling the whole universe. To this we reply that the liberated get all the powers except that of ruling the universe. Ruling the universe is guiding the form and the life and the desires of all the sentient and the non-sentient beings, excepting the liberated ones from whom all that veils His true nature has been removed, and who enjoy the glory of the unobstructed perception of the *Brahman*. This is proved from the scriptural text, 'From whom all these things are born, by whom all that are born live, unto whom they, departing, return; ask about It, That is *Brahman*.' If this quality of ruling the universe be a quality common even to the liberated, then this text would not apply as a definition of *Brahman*, defining Him through His rulership of the universe. The uncommon alone has to be specially defined; therefore, 'My beloved boy, alone, in the beginning, there existed the One without a second. That saw and felt I will give birth to the many. That projected heat.' '*Brahman*, indeed, alone existed in the beginning. That One evolved. That projected a blessed form, the Kshatra. All these gods are *Kshatras: Varuna, Soma, Rudra, Parjanya, Yama, Mrityu, Îśâna*.' '*Âtman*, indeed, existed alone in the beginning; nothing else vibrated; He, seeing, projected the world; He projected the world after.' 'Alone *Nârâyana* existed; neither *Brahmâ* nor *Îśâna*, nor the *Dyâvâ-Prithvî*, nor the stars, nor water, nor fire, nor Soma nor the Sun. He did not take pleasure alone. He after His meditation had one daughter, the ten organs, etc.,' in texts like these and others as, 'Who living in the earth is separate from the earth, who living in the *Âtman*, etc.,' the *Śrutis* speak of the Supreme One as the subject of the work of ruling the universe......Nor in these descriptions of the ruling of the universe is there any position of the liberated soul by which such a soul may have the ruling of the universe ascribed to it. In explaining the next *Sûtrâ*, Râmânuja says, "If you say it is not so, because there are direct texts in the Vedas in evidence to the contrary, these texts refer to the glory of the liberated in the spheres of the subordinate deities." This also is an easy solution of the difficulty. Although the system of Râmânuja admits the unity of the total, within that totality of existence there are, according to him, eternal differences. Therefore, for all practical purposes, this system also being dualistic, it was easy for Râmânuja to keep up the distinction between the personal soul and the personal God very clearly.

We will now try to understand what the great representative of the *Adwaita* School has got to say on the point. We shall see how the *Adwaita* system maintains all the hopes and aspirations of the dualist intact, and at the same time propounds its own solution of the problem, in consonance with the high destiny of divine humanity. Those, who aspire to retain their individual mind even after liberation, and to remain distinct will have ample opportunity of realising their aspiration and enjoy the blessing of the qualified Brahman. These are they who have been spoken of in the *Bhâgavata Purâna* thus: "O king, such are the glorious qualities of the Lord that the sages whose only pleasure is in the Self, and from whom all bondages have fallen off, even they love the Omni-Present with the love that is for love's sake." These are they who are spoken of by the *Sânkhyas* as getting merged in nature in this cycle so that, after attaining perfection, they may come out in the next as lords of world-systems. But none of these ever becomes equal to God *(Îśvara)*. Those who attain to that state where there is neither creation, nor created, nor creator, where there is neither knower, nor knowable, nor knowledge, where there is neither *I*, nor *thou*, nor *he*, where there is neither subject, nor object, nor relation, "there, who is seen by whom?" such persons have gone beyond everything, beyond "where words cannot go nor mind," gone to that which the *Śrutîs* declare as "Not this, Not this;" but for those who cannot, or will not reach this state, there will inevitably remain the triune vision of the one undifferentiated *Brahman* as nature, soul, and the interpenetrating sustainer of both *Îśvara*. So, when *Prahlâda* forgot himself, he found neither the universe nor its cause; all was to him one Infinite, undifferentiated by name and form; but as soon as he remembered that he was *Prahlâda* there was the universe before him and with it the Lord of the universe "the repository of an infinite number of blessed qualities." So, it was with the blessed *Gopîs*. So long as they had lost sense of their own personal identity and individuality, they were all *Krishnas*, and when they began again to think of him as the One to be worshipped, then they were *Gopîs* again, and immediately "Unto them appeared Krishna with smile on his lotus face, clad in yellow robes and having garlands on, the embodied conqueror (in beauty) of the god of love." (*Bhâgavata Purâna*).

Now to go back to our *Âchârya Śankara*: "Those," he says, "who by worshipping the qualified *Brahman* attain conjunction with the Supreme Ruler preserving their own mind is their glory limited or unlimited? This doubt arising, we get as an argument: Their glory should be unlimited, because of the scriptural texts 'They attain their own kingdom' 'To him all the gods offer worship' 'Their desires are fulfilled in all the worlds.' As an answer to this, *Vyâsâ* writes 'Without the power of ruling the universe.' Barring the power of creation, etc., of the universe, the other powers such as *animâ*, etc., are acquired by the liberated. As to ruling the universe, that belongs to the eternally perfect *Îśvara*. Why? Because He is the subject of all the scriptural texts as regards creation, etc., and the liberated souls are not mentioned in any connection with creation, etc. The Supreme Lord, indeed, is alone engaged in ruling the universe. The texts as to creation, etc., all point to Him. Also, there is given the adjective "ever perfect." Also, the scriptures say that the powers *animâ*, etc., of others are from the search after, and the worship of, God. Therefore, they have no place in the ruling of the universe. Again, on account of their possessing their own minds it is possible that their wills may differ, and that, whilst one desires creation, another may desire destruction. The only way of avoiding this conflict is to make all wills subordinate to someone will. Therefore, the conclusion is that the wills of the liberated are dependent on the will of the Supreme Ruler."

Bhakti, then, can be directed towards *Brahman*, only in his personal aspect. "The way is more difficult for those, whose mind is attached to the Absolute!" *Bhakti* has to float on smoothly with the current of our nature. True it is that we cannot have any idea of the *Brahman*, which is not anthropomorphic, but is it not equally true of everything we know? The greatest psychologist the world has ever known, Bhagavân Kapila, demonstrated ages ago that human consciousness is one of the elements in the make-up of all the objects of our perception and conception, internal as well as external. Beginning with our own bodies and going up to *Îśvara* we may see that every object of our perception is this consciousness plus a something else, whatever that may be; and this unavoidable mixture is what we ordinarily think of as reality. Indeed, it is, and ever will be, all of the reality that is possible for the human mind to know. Therefore, to say that *Îśvara* is unreal, because He is anthropomorphic, is sheer nonsense. It sounds very much like the occidental squabble on idealism and realism, which fearful-looking quarrel has for its foundation a mere play on the word *real*. The idea of *Îśvara* covers all the ground ever denoted and connoted by the word real, and *Îśvara* is as much real as anything else in the universe; and after all the word real means nothing more than what has now been pointed out. Such is our philosophical conception of *Îśvara*.

III. Spiritual Realisation, The Aim Of Bhakti-Yoga

To the *Bhakta* these dry details are necessary only to strengthen his will; beyond that they are of no use to him. For he is treading on a path which is fitted very soon to lead him beyond the hazy and turbulent regions of reason, to lead him to the realm of realisation. He, soon, through the mercy of the Lord, reaches a plane where pedantic and powerless reason is left far behind, and the mere intellectual groping through the dark gives place to the daylight of direct perception. He no more reasons and believes, he almost perceives. He no more argues, he senses. And is not this seeing God, and feeling God, and enjoying God, higher than everything else? Nay, *Bhaktas* have not been wanting who have maintained that it is higher than even *Moksha* liberation. And is it not also the highest utility? There are people and a good many of them, too in the world who are convinced that only that is of use and utility which brings to man creature-comforts. Even Religion, God, Eternity, Soul, none of these is of any use to them, as they do not bring them money or physical comfort. To such all those things, which do not gratify the senses and appease the appetites, are of no utility. In every mind, utility, however, is conditioned by its own peculiar wants. To men, therefore, who never rise higher than eating, drinking, begetting progeny, and dying, the only gain is in sense enjoyments; and they must wait and go through many more births and re-incarnations to learn to feel even the faintest necessity for anything higher. But those to whom the eternal interests of the soul are of much higher value than the fleeting interests of this mundane life, to whom the gratification of the senses is but like the thoughtless play of the baby, to them God and the love of God form the highest and the only utility of human existence. Thank God there are some such still living in this world of too much worldliness.

Bhakti-Yoga, as we have said, is divided into the gaunî or the preparatory, and the *parâ* or the supreme forms. We shall find, as we go on, how, in the preparatory stage, we unavoidably stand in need of many concrete helps to enable us to get on; and, indeed, the mythological and symbological parts of all religions are natural growths which early environ the aspiring soul and help it Godward. It is also a significant fact that spiritual giants have been produced only in those systems of religion where there is an exuberant growth of rich mythology and ritualism. The dry fanatical forms of religion which attempt to eradicate all that is poetical, all that is beautiful and sublime, all that gives a firm grasp to the infant mind tottering in its Godward way the forms which attempt to break down the very ridge poles of the spiritual roof, and in their ignorant and superstitious conceptions of truth try to drive away all that is life-giving, all that furnishes the formative material to the spiritual plant growing in the human soul such forms of religion too soon find that all of what is left to them is but an empty shell, a contentless frame of words and sophistry, with perhaps a little flavour of a kind of social scavenge ring or the so-called spirit of reform. The vast mass of those whose religion is like this are conscious or unconscious materialists the end and aim of their lives here and hereafter being enjoyment, which, indeed, is to them the alpha and the omega of human life. Work like street-cleaning and scavenge ring intended for the material comfort of man is, according to them, the "be-all" and "end-all" of human existence; and the sooner the followers of this curious mixture of ignorance and fanaticism come out in their true colours, and join, as they well deserve to do, the ranks of atheists and materialists, the better will it be for the world. One ounce of the practice of righteousness and of spiritual self-realisation out-weighs tons and tons of frothy talk and nonsensical sentiments. Show us one, but one, gigantic spiritual genius growing out of all this dry dust of ignorance and fanaticism; and if you cannot, close your mouths, open the windows of your hearts to the clear light of truth, and sit like children at the feet of those who know what they are talking about the sages of India. Let us then listen attentively to what they say.

IV. The Need Of A Guru

Every soul is destined to be perfect, and every being, in the end, will attain the state of perfection. Whatever we are now, is the result of our acts and thoughts in the past; and whatever we shall be in the future, will be the result of what we think and do now. But this, our shaping of our own destinies, does not preclude our receiving help from outside; nay, in the vast majority of cases such help is absolutely necessary. When it comes, the higher powers and possibilities of the soul are quickened, spiritual life is awakened, growth is animated, and man becomes holy and perfect in the end.

This quickening impulse cannot be derived from books. The soul can only receive impulses from another soul, and from nothing else. We may study books all our lives, we may become very intellectual; but, in the end, we find that we have not developed at all spiritually. It is not true that a high order of intellectual development always goes hand in hand with a proportionate development of the spiritual side in man. In studying books, we are sometimes deluded into thinking that thereby we are being spiritually helped; but, if we analyse the effect of the study of books on ourselves, we shall find that, at the utmost, it is only our intellect that derived profit from such studies, but not our inner spirit. This insufficiency of books to quicken spiritual growth is the reason why, although almost every one of us can *speak* most wonderfully on spiritual matters, when it comes to action and the living of a truly spiritual life, we find ourselves so awfully deficient. To quicken the spirit, the impulse must come from another soul.

The person from whose soul such impulse comes is called the *Guru*—the teacher; and the person to whose soul the impulse is conveyed is called the *Śishya*—the student. To convey such an impulse, to any soul, in the first place, the soul from which it proceeds must possess the power of transmitting it, as it were to another; and, in the second place, the soul to which it is transmitted must be fit to receive it. The seed must be a living seed, and the field must be ready ploughed; and when both these conditions are fulfilled a wonderful growth of genuine religion takes place. "The true preacher of religion has to be of wonderful capabilities, and clever shall his hearer be" and when both of these are really wonderful and extraordinary, then will a splendid spiritual awakening result, and not otherwise. Such alone are the real teachers, and such alone are also the real students, the real aspirants. All others are only playing with spirituality. They have just a little curiosity awakened, just a little intellectual aspiration kindled in them, but are merely standing on the outward fringe of the horizon of religion. There is, no doubt, some value even in that, as it may, in course of time, result, in the awakening of a real thirst for religion; and it is a mysterious law of nature that, as soon as the field is ready, the seed must and does come, as soon as the soul earnestly desires to have religion, the transmitter of the religious force must and does appear to help that soul. When the power that attracts the light of religion in the receiving soul is full and strong, the power which answers to that attraction and sends in light does come as a matter of course.

There are, however, certain great dangers in the way. There is, for instance, the danger to the receiving soul of its mistaking momentary emotions for real religious yearning. We may study that in ourselves. Many a time in our lives, somebody dies whom we loved; we receive a blow; we feel that the world is slipping between our fingers, that we want something surer and higher, and that we must become religious. In a few days that wave of feeling has passed away, and we are left stranded just where we were before. We are all of us often mistaking such impulses for real thirst after religion; but as long as these momentary emotions are thus mistaken, that continuous, real, craving of the soul for religion will not come, and we cannot find the true transmitter of spirituality into our nature. So, whenever we are tempted to complain of our search after the truth, that we desire so much, proving vain, instead of so complaining, our first duty ought to be to look into our own souls, and find whether the craving in the heart is real. Then in the vast majority of cases it would be discovered that we were not fit for receiving the truth, that there was no real thirst for spirituality.

There are still greater dangers in regard to the *transmitter*, the *Guru*. There are many who, though immersed in ignorance, yet, in the pride of their hearts, fancy they know everything, and not only do not stop there, but offer to take others on their shoulders; and thus, the blind leading the blind, both fall into the ditch. "Fools dwelling in darkness, wise in their own conceit, and puffed up with vain knowledge, go round and round staggering to and fro, like blind men led by the blind." (*Mund*. Up., 1. 2. 8). The world is full of these. Everyone wants to be a teacher; every beggar wants to make a gift of a million dollars! Just as these beggars are ridiculous, so are these teachers.

V. Qualifications Of The Aspirant And The Teacher

How are we to know a teacher then? The sun requires no torch to make him visible, we need not light a candle in order to see him. When the sun rises, we instinctively become aware of the fact, and when a teacher of men comes to help us, the soul will instinctively know that truth has already begun to shine upon it. Truth stands on its own evidence, it does not require any other testimony to prove it true, it is self-effulgent. It penetrates into the innermost corners of our nature, and in its presence the whole universe stands up and says, "This is truth." The teachers whose wisdom and truth shine like the light of the sun are the very greatest the world has known, and they are worshipped as gods by the major portion of mankind. But we may get help from comparatively lesser ones also; only we ourselves do not possess intuition enough to judge well of the man from whom we receive teaching and guidance; so, there ought to be certain tests, certain conditions, for the teacher to satisfy, as there are also for the taught.

The conditions necessary for the taught are purity, a real thirst after knowledge, and perseverance. No impure soul can be really religious. Purity in thought, speech, and act, is absolutely necessary for one to be religious. As to the thirst after knowledge, it is an old law that we all get whatever we want. None of us can get anything other than what we fix our hearts upon. To pant for religion truly is a very difficult thing, not at all so easy as we generally imagine. Hearing religious talks, reading religious books, is no proof yet of a real want felt in the heart; there must be a continuous struggle, a constant fight, an unremitting grappling with our lower nature, till the higher want is actually felt and the victory is achieved. It is not a question of one or two days, of years, or of lives; the struggle may have to go on for hundreds of lifetimes. The success sometimes may come immediately, but we must be ready to wait patiently even for what may look like an infinite length of time. The student who sets out with such a spirit of perseverance will surely find success and realisation at last.

In regard to the teacher, we must see that he knows the spirit of the scriptures. The whole world reads Bibles, Vedas, and Qurans; but they are all only words, syntax, etymology, philology, the dry bones of religion. The teacher who deals too much in words and allows the mind to be carried away by the force of words, loses the spirit. It is the knowledge of the *spirit* of the scriptures alone that constitutes the true religious teacher. The network of the words of the scriptures is like a huge forest in which the human mind often loses itself and finds no way out. "The network of words is a big forest; it is the cause of curious wanderings." The various methods of joining words, the various methods of speaking in beautiful language, the various methods of explaining the diction of the scriptures, are only for the disputations and enjoyment of the learned; they do not conduce to the development of spiritual conception. Those who employ such methods to impart religion to others are only desirous to show off their learning, so that the world may praise them as great scholars. You will find that no one of the great teachers of the world ever went into these various explanations of the texts, there is with them no attempt at "text torturing," no eternal playing upon the meaning of words and their roots. Yet they nobly taught, while others who have nothing to teach, have taken up a word sometimes, and written a three-volume book on its origin, on the man who used it first, and on what that man was accustomed to eat, and how long he slept and so on.

Bhagavân Râmakrishna used to tell a story of some men who went into a mango orchard and busied themselves in counting the leaves, the twigs, and the branches, examining their colour, comparing their and noting down everything most carefully, and then got up a learned discussion on each of these topics which were undoubtedly highly interesting to them. But one of them, more sensible than the others, did not care for all these things, and instead thereof, began to eat the mango fruit. And was he not wise? So, leave this counting of leaves and twigs and this note-taking to others. This kind of work has its proper place, but not here in the spiritual domain. You can never once see a strong spiritual man among these "leaf-counters." Religion, the highest aim, the highest glory of man, does not require so much labour as *leaf-counting*, If you want to be *Bhakta* it is not at all necessary for you to know where *Krishna* was born, in *Mathurâ* or in *Vraja*, what he was doing, or just the exact date on which he pronounced the teachings of the *Gîtâ*. You only require to feel the craving for the beautiful lessons of duty and love in the *Gîtâ*. All the other particulars about it and its author are for the enjoyment of the learned. Let them have what they desire. Say *"Śantih Śantih"* to their learned controversies and let us eat the mangoes.

The second condition necessary in the teacher is sinlessness. The question is often asked, "Why should we look into the character and personality of a teacher? We have only to judge of what he says and take that up." This is not right. If a man wants to teach me something of dynamics or chemistry, or any other physical science, he may be anything he likes, because what the physical sciences require, is merely an intellectual equipment; but in the spiritual sciences it is impossible from first to last that there can be any spiritual light in the soul that is impure. What religion can an impure man teach? The *sine qua non* of acquiring spiritual truth for one's self, or for imparting it to others, is the purity of heart and soul. A vision of God, or a glimpse of the beyond, never comes until the soul is pure. Hence with the teacher of religion we must see first what he *is*, and then what he says. He must be perfectly pure, and then alone comes the value of his words, because he is only then the true "transmitter." What can he transmit, if he has not spiritual power in himself? There must be the worthy vibration of spirituality in the mind of the teacher so that it may be sympathetically conveyed to the mind of the taught. The function of the teacher is indeed an affair of the transference of something, and not one of a mere stimulation of the existing intellectual or other faculties in the taught. Something real and appreciable as an influence comes from the teacher and goes to the taught. Therefore, the teacher must be pure.

The third condition is in regard to the motive. The teacher must not teach with any ulterior selfish motive, for money, name, or fame; his work must be simply out of love, out of pure love for mankind at large. The only medium through which spiritual force can be transmitted is love. Any selfish motive, such as the desire for gain or for name, will immediately destroy this conveying medium. God is love, and only he who has known God as love can be a teacher of godliness and God to man.

When you see that in your teacher these conditions are all fulfilled, you are safe; if they are not, it is unsafe to allow yourself to be taught by him, for there is the great danger that, if he cannot convey goodness into your heart, he may convey wickedness. This danger must by all means be guarded against. "He who is learned, sinless and unpolluted by lust is the greatest knower of the *Brahman*."

From what has been said, it naturally follows that we cannot be taught to love, appreciate, and assimilate religion everywhere and by everybody. The "sermon in stones, books in running brooks, and good in everything" is all very true as a poetical figure: but no man can impart to another a single grain of truth unless he has the undeveloped germs of it in himself. To whom do the stones and brooks preach sermons? To the human soul the lotus of whose inner holy shrine is already quick with life. And the light which causes the beautiful opening out of this lotus comes always from the good and wise teacher. When the heart has thus been opened, It becomes fit to receive teaching from the stones, or the brooks, or the stars, or the sun, or the moon, or from anything which has its existence in our divine universe; but the unopened heart will see in them nothing but mere stones or mere brooks. A blind man may go to a museum, but he will not profit by it in any way; his eyes must be opened first, and then alone he will be able to learn what the things in the museum can teach.

This eye-opener of the aspirant after religion is the teacher. With the teacher, therefore, our relationship is the same as that between an ancestor and his descendant. Without faith, humility, submission, and veneration in our hearts to our religious teacher, there cannot be any growth of religion in us; and it is a significant fact that, where this kind of relation between the teacher and the taught prevails, there alone gigantic spiritual men are growing, while in those countries which have neglected to keep up this kind of relation, the religious teacher has become a mere lecturer, the teacher expecting his five dollars, and the person taught expecting his brain to be filled with the teacher's words, and each going his own way after this much is done. Under such circumstances spirituality becomes almost an unknown quantity. There is none to transmit it, and none to have it transmitted to. Religion with such people becomes business, they think they can obtain it with their dollars. Would to God that religion could be obtained so easily! But unfortunately, it cannot.

Religion, which is the highest knowledge and the highest wisdom, cannot be bought, nor can it be acquired from books. You may thrust your head into all the corners of the world, you may explore the Himalayas, the Alps, and the Caucasus, you may sound the bottom of the sea, and pry into every nook of Thibet and the desert of Gobi, you will not find it anywhere, until your heart is ready for receiving it, and your teacher has come. And when that divinely appointed teacher comes, serve him with childlike confidence and simplicity, freely open your heart to his influence, and see in him God manifested. Those who come to seek truth with such a spirit of love and veneration, to them the Lord of Truth reveals the most wonderful things regarding Truth, Goodness, and Beauty.

VI. Incarnate Teachers And Incarnation

Wherever His name is spoken, that very place is holy. How much more so is the man who speaks His name, and with what veneration ought we to approach that man out of whom comes to us spiritual truth? Such great teachers of spiritual truth are indeed very few in number in this world, but the world is never altogether without them. The moment it is absolutely bereft of these, it becomes a hideous hell and hastens on to its destruction. They are always the fairest flowers of human life, the ocean of mercy without any motive. "Know the *Guru* to be Me," says Śrî Krishna in the Gîtâ.

Higher and nobler than all ordinary ones are another set of teachers, *Avatâras* of *Îśvara* in the world. They can transmit spirituality with a touch, even with a mere wish. The lowest and the most degraded characters become in one second saints at their command. They are the Teachers of all teachers, the highest manifestations of God through man. We cannot see God except through them. We cannot help worshipping them; and indeed, they are the only ones whom we are bound to worship.

No man can really see God except through these human

manifestations. If we try to see God otherwise, we make for ourselves a hideous caricature of Him, and believe the caricature to be no worse than the original. There is a story of an ignorant man who was asked to make an image of the God Siva, and who, after days of hard struggle, manufactured only the image of a monkey! So, whenever we try to think of God as He is in His absolute perfection, we invariably meet with the most miserable failure; because as long as we are men, we cannot conceive Him as anything higher than man. The time will come when we shall transcend our human nature and know Him as He is; but as long as we are men, we must worship Him in man and as man. Talk as you may, try as you may, you cannot think of God except as a man. You may deliver great intellectual discourses on God and all things under the sun, become very great rationalists and prove to your satisfaction that all these accounts of the *Avatâras* of God as man are nonsense. But let us come for a moment to practical common sense. What is there behind this kind of remarkable intellect? Zero, nothing, simply so much froth. When next you hear a man delivering a great intellectual lecture against this worship of the *Avatâras* of God, get hold of him and ask him what *his* idea of God is, what he knows by "omnipotence," "omnipresence," and all similar terms, beyond the spelling of the words. He really means nothing by them; he cannot formulate as their meaning any idea unaffected by his own human nature; he is no better off in this matter than the man in the street who has not read a single book. That man in the street, however, is quiet and does not disturb the peace of the world, while this big talker creates disturbance and misery among mankind. Religion is after all realisation, and we must make the sharpest distinction between talk and intuitive experience. What we experience in the depths of our souls is realisation. Nothing indeed is so uncommon as common sense in regard to this matter.

By our present constitution we are limited and bound to see

God as man. If, for instance, the buffaloes want to worship God, they will, in keeping with their own nature, see Him as a huge buffalo; if a fish wants to worship God, it will have to form an idea of Him as a big fish; and man has to think of Him as man. And these various conceptions are not due to morbidly active imagination. Man, the buffalo, and the fish, all may be supposed to represent so many different vessels so to say. All these vessels go to the sea of God to get filled with water, each according to its own shape and capacity; in the man the water takes the shape of man, in the buffalo the shape of a buffalo, and in the fish the shape of the fish. In each of these vessels there is the same water of the sea of God. When men see Him, they see Him as man, and the animals, if they have any conception of God at all, must see Him as animal, each according to its own ideal. So, we cannot help seeing God as man, and, therefore, we are bound to worship Him as man. There is no other way.

Two kinds of men do not worship God as man the human brute who has no religion, and the *Paramahamsa*, who has risen beyond all the weaknesses of humanity and has transcended the limits of his own human nature. To him all nature has become his own Self. He alone can worship God as He is. Here too, as in all other cases, the two extremes meet. The extreme of ignorance and the other extreme of knowledge neither of these go through acts of worship. The human brute does not worship because of his ignorance, and the *Jîvanmuktas* (free souls) do not worship because they have realised God in themselves. Being between these two poles of existence, if anyone tells you that he is not going to worship God as man, take kindly care of, that man; he is, not to use any harsher term, an irresponsible talker; his religion is for unsound and empty brains.

God understands human failings and becomes man to do good to humanity. "Whenever virtue subsides and wickedness prevails, I manifest myself. To establish virtue, to destroy evil, to save the good I come from *yuga* to *yuga*." "Fools deride me who have assumed the human form, without knowing my real nature as the Lord of the universe." Such is *Śrî Krishna's* declaration in the Gita on incarnation. "When a huge tidal wave comes," says Bhagavân *Śrî Râmakrishna*, "all the little brooks and ditches become full to the brim without any effort or consciousness on their own part; so, when an incarnation comes a tidal wave of spirituality breaks upon the world, and people feel spirituality almost full in the air."

VII. The Mantra: Om: Word And Wisdom

But we are now considering not these *Mahâ-purushas*, the great incarnations, but only the *Siddha-Gurus* (teachers who have attained the goal); they as a rule have to convey the germs of spiritual wisdom to the disciple by means of words (*mantra*) to be meditated upon. What are these *mantras*? The whole of this universe has, according to Indian philosophy, both name and form as its conditions of manifestation. In the human microcosm, there cannot be a single wave in the mind-stuff (chitta), unconditioned by name and form. If it be true that nature is built throughout on the same plan, this kind of conditioning by name and form must also be the plan of the building of the whole of the cosmos. "As one lump of clay being known, all clay is known," so the knowledge of the microcosm must lead to the knowledge of the macrocosm. Now, form is the outer crust, of which the name or the idea is the inner essence or kernel. The body is the form, and the mind, or the *antahkarana*, is the name, and sound-symbols are universally associated with name in all beings having the power of speech. In the individual man the thought-waves arising in the limited mahat or mind-stuff (chitta) must manifest themselves, first as words, and then as the more concrete forms.

In the universe, Brahma or *Hiranya-garbha*, or the cosmic intelligence (mahat) first manifested himself as name, and then as form, *i. e.*, as this universe. All this expressed sensible universe is the form, behind which stands the eternal inexpressible *sphota* the manifestor as *Logos* or Word. This eternal *sphota*, the essential eternal material of all ideas or names, is the power through which the Lord creates the universe; nay, the Lord first becomes conditioned as the *sphota*, and then evolves himself out as the yet more concrete sensible universe. This *sphota*, has one word as its only possible symbol, and this is the *Om*. And as by no possible means of analysis we can separate the word from the idea, this *Om* and the eternal *sphota* are inseparable; and therefore, it is out of this holiest of all holy words, the mother of all names and forms, the eternal *Om*, that the whole universe may be supposed to have been created. But it may be said that, although thought and word are inseparable, yet as there may be various word-symbols for the same thought, it is not necessary that this particular word *Om* should be the word representative of the thought, out of which the universe has become manifested. To this objection we reply that this *Om* is the only possible symbol which covers the whole ground, and there is none other like it. The *sphota* is the material of all words yet is not any definite word in its fully formed state. That is to say, if all the peculiarities which distinguish one word from another be removed, then what remains will be the *sphota*; therefore, this *sphota* is called the *Nâda-Brahma* (the sound-*Brahman*). Now, as every word-symbol, intended to express the inexpressible *sphota* will so particularize it that it will no longer be the *sphota*, that symbol which particularizes it the least and at the same time most approximately expresses its nature, will be the truest symbol thereof; and this is the *Om*, and the *Om* only; because these three letters A, U, M, pronounced in combination as *Om*, may well be the generalised symbol of all possible sounds. The letter A is the least differentiated of all sounds, therefore Krishna says in the Gîtâ "I am A among the letters." Again, all articulate sounds are produced in the space within the mouth beginning with the root of the tongue and ending in the lips the throat sound is A, and M is the last lip sound; and the U exactly represents the rolling forward of the impulse which begins at the root of the tongue till it ends in the lips. If properly pronounced, this *Om* will represent the whole phenomenon of sound-production, and no other word can do this; and this, therefore, is the fittest symbol of the *sphota*, which is the real meaning of the *Om*. And as the symbol can never be separated from the thing signified, the *Om* and the *sphota* are one. And as the *sphota*, being the finer side of the manifested universe, is nearer to God, and is indeed the first manifestation of Divine Wisdom, this *Om* is truly symbolic of God. Again, just as the "one only" *Brahman*, the *Akhanda Satchiddnanda*, the undivided Existence-Knowledge-Bliss, can be conceived by imperfect human souls only from particular standpoints of view and associated with particular qualities, so this universe, His body, has also to be thought of along the line of the thinker's mind.

This direction of the worshipper's mind is guided by its prevailing elements or *Tattvas*. The result is that the same God will be seen in various manifestations as the possessor of various predominant qualities, and the same universe will appear as full of manifold forms. In the same way in which, even in the case of the least differentiated and the most universal symbol *Om*, thought and sound-symbol are seen to be inseparably associated with each other, this law of their inseparable association applies to the many differentiated views of God and the universe: each of them must have a particular word-symbol to express it. These word-symbols, evolved out of the deepest spiritual perceptions of sages, symbolize and express as nearly as possible the particular view of God and the universe they stand for. And as the *Om* represents the *Akhanda*, the undifferentiated *Brahman*, the others represent the *Khanda* or the differentiated views of the same Being; and they are all helpful to divine meditation and the acquisition of true knowledge.

VIII. Worship Of Substitutes And Images

The next points to be considered are the worship of *Pratîkâs* or of things more or less satisfactory as substitutes for God, and the worship of *Pratîmâs* or images. What is the worship of God through a *Pratîkâ*? It is "Joining the mind with devotion to that which is not *Brahman*, taking it to be *Brahman*." Says *Bhagavân Râmânuja*: "Worship the mind as *Brahman*, this is internal; and the *Âkâśa* as *Brahman*, this is the sense-meaning." The mind is an internal *Pratîkâ*, the *Âkâśa* is an external one; and both have to be worshipped as substitutes of God. Similarly, "The Sun is *Brahman*, this is the command'...... 'He who worships Name as *Brahman*,' and in all such passages the doubt arises as to the worship of *Pratîkâs*......," says Śankara. The word *Pratîkâ* means going towards, and worshipping a *Pratîkâ* is worshipping something which as a substitute, is, in some one or more respects, like the *Brahman* more and more, but is not the *Brahman*. Along with the *Pratîkâs* mentioned in the *Śrutis* there are various others to be found in the *Purânas* and the *Tantras*. In this kind of *Pratîkâ-worship* may be included all the various forms of *Pitri-worship* and *Deva-worship*.

Now worshipping Îśvara and Him alone is *Bhakti*; the worship of anything else, *Deva*, or *Pitri*, or any other being cannot be *Bhakti*. The various kinds of worship of the various *Devas* are all to be included in ritualistic *Karma*, which gives to the worshipper only a particular result in the form of some celestial enjoyment but can neither give rise to *Bhakti* nor lead to *Mukti*. One thing, therefore, has to be carefully borne in mind. If, as it may happen in some cases, the highly philosophic ideal supreme *Brahman* is Himself dragged down by *Pratîkâ-worship* to the level of the *Pratîkâ*, and the *Pratîkâ* itself is taken to be the *Âtman* of the worshipper, or his *Antarayâmin*, the worshipper gets entirely misled, as no *Pratîkâ* can really be the *Âtman* of the worshipper. But where *Brahman* Himself is the object of worship, and the *Pratîkâ* stands only as a substitute or a suggestion thereof, that is to say, where through the *Pratîkâ* the omnipresent *Brahman* is worshipped the *Pratîkâ* itself being idealized into the cause of all, the *Brahman* the worship is positively beneficial; nay, it is absolutely necessary for all mankind, until they have all got beyond the primary or preparatory state of the mind in regard to worship. When, therefore, any gods or other beings are worshipped in and for themselves, such worship is only a ritualistic *Karma*; and as a *Vidyâ* (science) it gives us only the fruit belonging to that particular *Vidyâ*; but when the *Devas* or any other beings are looked upon as *Brahman* and worshipped, the result obtained is the same as by the worshipping of *Îśvara*. This explains how, in many cases, both in the *Śrutis* and the *Smritis*, a god, or a sage, or some other extraordinary being is taken up and lifted, as it were, out of its own nature and idealized into *Brahman*, and is then worshipped. Says the *Advaitin*, "Is not everything *Brahman* when the name and the form have been removed from it." "Is not He, the Lord, the innermost self of everyone?" says the *Visishtâdvaitin*. "The fruition of even the worship of the *Âdityas*, etc, *Brahman* Himself bestows, because he is the Ruler of all," says Śankara in his *Brahma-Sutra-Bhashya*. "Here in this way does *Brahman* become the object of worship, because He, as *Brahman*, is superposed on the *Pratîkâs*, just as Vishnu, etc., are superposed upon images, etc."

The same ideas apply to the worship of the *Pratîmâs* as do to that of the *Pratîkâs*; that is to say, if the image stands for a god or a saint, the worship is not the result of *Bhakti*, and does not lead to liberation; but if it stands for the one God, the worship thereof will bring both *Bhakti* and *Mukti*. Of the principal religions of the world we see Vedântism, Buddhism, and certain forms of Christianity freely using images; only two religions, Mahomedanism and Protestanism, refuse such help. Yet the Mahomedans use the graves of their saints and martyrs almost in the place of images; the Protestants, in rejecting all concrete helps to religion, are drifting away every year farther and farther from spirituality, and at present there is scarcely any difference between the advanced Protestants and the followers of Auguste Comte, or the Agnostics who preach ethics alone. Again, in Christianity and Mahomedanism whatever exists of image-worship is made to fall under that category in which the *Pratîkâ* or the *Pratîmâ* is worshipped in itself but not as a "help to the vision" of God; therefore, it is at best only of the nature of ritualistic *Karmas* and cannot produce either *Bhakti* or *Mukti*. In this form of image worship, the allegiance of the soul is given to other things than *Îśvara*, and, therefore, such use of images or graves, of temples or tombs, is real idolatry; yet it is in itself neither sinful nor wicked it is a rite a *Karma*, and worshippers must and will get the fruit thereof.

IX. The Chosen Ideal

The next thing to be considered is what we know as *Ishta Nishthâ*. One who aspires to be a *Bhakta* must know that "so many opinions are so many ways." He must know that all the various sects of the various religions are the various manifestations of the glory of the same Lord. "They call You by so many names; they divide You, as it were, by different names, yet in each one of these is to be found Your omnipotence......

You reach the worshipper through all of these; neither is there any specialty of time so long as the soul has intense love for You...You are so easy of approach; it is my misfortune that I cannot love You." Not only this, the *Bhakta* must take care not to hate, nor even to criticize, those radiant sons of light who are the founders of various sects; he has not even to hear them spoken ill of. Very few, indeed, are those who are at once the possessors of an extensive sympathy and power of appreciation as well as an intensity of love. We find as a rule that liberal and sympathetic sects lose the intensity of religious feeling, and in their hands, religion is apt to degenerate into a kind of politico-social club life. On the other hand, intensely narrow sectaries, whilst displaying a very commendable love of their own ideals, are seen to have acquired every particle of that love by hating everyone who is not exactly of the same opinion as they are. Would to God that this world was full of men who were as intense in their love as world-wide in their sympathies! But such are only few and far between. Yet we know that it is practicable to educate large numbers of human beings into the ideal of a wonderful blending of both the width and intensity of love; and the way to do that is by this path of the *Ishta Nishthá* or the "chosen ideal." Every sect of every religion presents only one ideal of its own to mankind, but the eternal Vedântic religion opens to mankind an infinite number of doors for ingress into the inner shrine of Divinity, and places before humanity an almost inexhaustible array of ideals, there being in each of them a manifestation of the Eternal One. With the kindest solicitude the Vedânta points out to aspiring men and women the numerous roads hewn out of the solid rock of the realities of human life by the glorious sons, or human manifestations, of God in the past and in the present, and stands with outstretched arms to welcome all, to welcome even those that are yet to be to that Home of Truth and that Ocean of Bliss wherein the human soul liberated out of the net of Mâyâ may transport itself with perfect freedom and with eternal joy.

Bhakti-Yoga, therefore, lays on us the imperative command not to hate or deny anyone of the various paths that lead to salvation. Yet the growing plant must be hedged around to protect it until it has grown into a tree. The tender plant of spirituality will die if exposed too early to the action of a constant change of ideas and ideals. Many people, in the name of what may be called religious liberalism, may be seen to be feeding their idle curiosity with a continuous succession of different ideals. With them hearing new things grows into a sort of disease, a sort of religious drink-mania. They want to hear new things just to get a sort of temporary nervous excitement, and, when one such exciting influence has had its effect on them, they are ready for another. Religion is with these people a sort of intellectual opium-eating, and there it ends. "There is another sort of men," says *Bhagavân Râmakrishna*, "who are like the pearl oyster of the story. The pearl oyster leaves its bed at the bottom of the sea and comes up to the surface to catch the rainwater when the star *Svâti* is in the ascendant. It floats about on the surface of the sea with its shell wide open until it has succeeded in catching a drop of the rainwater, and then it dives deep down to its seabed and there rests until it has succeeded in fashioning a beautiful pearl out of that rain drop."

This is indeed the most poetical and forcible way in which the theory of I*shta Nishthâ* has ever been put. This *Eka Nishthâ*, or devotion to one ideal is absolutely necessary for the beginner in the practice of religious devotion. He must say with Hanuman in the Râmâyana "Though I know that the Lord of Srî and the Lord of Jânâkî are one and the same manifestation of the same Supreme Being, yet my all in all is the lotus-eyed Râmâ;" or, as was said by the sage Tulasîdâs, he must say "Take the sweetness of all, sit with all, take the name of all, say yea, yea, but keep your seat firm." Then, if the devotional aspirant is sincere, out of this little seed will come a gigantic tree like the Indian banyan, sending branch after branch and root after root to all sides, till it covers the entire field of religion. Thus, will the true devotee realize that He who was his own ideal in life is worshipped in all ideals by all sects, under all names, and through all forms.

X. The Method And The Means

In regard to the method and the means of *Bhakti Yoga* we read in the commentary of *Bhagavân Râmânuja* on the *Vedânta Sûtras:* "The attaining of That comes through discrimination, controlling the passions, practice, sacrificial work, purity, strength, and suppression of excessive joy." *Viveka* or discrimination is, according to *Râmânuja*, the discriminating, among other things, the pure food from the impure. According to him, food becomes impure from three causes: namely, (1) by the nature of the food itself, as in the case of garlic, etc.; (2) owing to its coming from wicked and accursed persons; and (3) from physical impurities, such as dirt, or hair, etc. The Srutis say, "When the food is pure the *Sattva* element gets purified, the memory becomes unwavering," and Râmânuja quotes this from the *Chhândogya Upanishad*.

The question of food has always been one of the most vital with the *Bhaktas*. Apart from the extravagance into which some of the *Bhakti* sects have run, there is a great truth underlying this question of food. We must remember that, according to the *Sânkhya* philosophy the *sattva, rajas,* and *tamas,* which in the state of homogeneous equilibrium form the *Prakriti* and in the heterogenous disturbed condition form the universe, are both the substance and the quality of *Prakriti*. As such they are the materials out of which every human form has been manufactured, and the predominance of the *sattva* material is what is absolutely necessary for spiritual development. The materials which we receive through our food into our body-structure go a great way to determine our mental constitution; therefore, the food we eat has to be particularly taken care of. However, in this matter as in others, the fanaticism into which the disciples invariably fall is not to be laid at the door of the masters.

And this discrimination of food is after all of secondary importance. The very same passage quoted above is explained by Śankara in his *Bhâshya* on the *Upanishads* in a different way by giving an entirely different meaning to the word *âhâra*, translated generally as food. According to him, "That which is gathered in is *âhâra*. The knowledge of the sensations such as sound, etc., is gathered in for the enjoyment of the enjoyer (Self); the purification of the knowledge which gathers in the perception of the senses is the purifying of the food (*âhâra*). The word 'purification-of-food' means the acquiring of the knowledge of sensations untouched by the defects of attachment, aversion, and delusion; such is the meaning. Therefore, such knowledge or *âhâra* being purified the *sattva* material of the possessor of it the internal organ will become purified, and the *sattva* being purified an unbroken memory of the infinite One who has been known in His real nature will result."

These two explanations are apparently conflicting, yet both are true and necessary. The manipulating and controlling of what may be called the finer body, *viz.*, the mind, are no doubt higher functions than the controlling of the grosser body of flesh. But the control of the grosser is absolutely necessary to enable one to arrive at the control of the finer. The beginner, therefore, must pay particular attention to all such dietetic rules as have come down from the line of his accredited teachers; but the extravagant, meaningless fanaticism, which has driven religion entirely to the kitchen, as may be noticed in the case of many of our sects, without any hope of the noble truth of that religion ever coming out to the sunlight of spirituality, is a peculiar sort of pure and simple materialism. It is neither *Gnâna*, nor *Bhakti*, nor *Karma*; it is a special kind of lunacy, and those who pin their souls to it are more likely to go to lunatic asylums than to *Brahma loka*. So, it stands to reason that discrimination in the choice of food is necessary for the attainment of this higher state of mental composition which cannot be easily obtained otherwise.

Controlling the passions is the next thing to be attended to. To restrain the *Indriyas* (organs) from going towards the objects of the senses, to control them and bring them under the guidance of the will is the very central virtue in religious culture. Then comes the practice of self-restraint and self-denial. All the immense possibilities of divine realisation in the soul cannot get actualised without struggle and without such practice on the part of the aspiring devotee. "The mind must always think of the Lord." It is very hard at first to compel the mind to think of the Lord always, but with every new effort the power to do so grows stronger in us. "By practice, oh son of Kunti, and by non-attachment is It attained," says Śrî Krishna in the Gîtâ.

Purity is absolutely the basic work, the bed-rock upon which the whole *Bhakti-building* rests. Cleansing the external body and discriminating the food are both easy, but without internal cleanliness and without purity, these external observances are of no value whatsoever. In the list of the qualities conducive to purity, as given by Râmânuja, there are enumerated, *Satya*, truthfulness; *Ârjava*, sincerity; *Dayâ*, doing good to others without any gain to one's self; *Ahimsâ*, not injuring others by thought or word or deed; *Abhidhyâ*, not coveting other's goods, not thinking vain thoughts, and not brooding over injuries received from another. In this list the one idea that deserves special notice is *Ahimsâ*, non-injury to others. This duty of non-injury, so to speak of it, is obligatory on us in relation to all beings; as with some, it does not simply mean the not-injuring of human beings and mercilessness towards the lower animals; nor, as with some others, does it mean the protecting of cats and dogs and the feeding of ants with sugar, with liberty to injure brother man in every horrible way. It is remarkable that almost every good idea in this world can be carried to a disgusting extreme. A good practice carried to an extreme and worked in accordance with the letter of the law becomes a positive evil.

The test of *Ahimsâ* is absence of jealousy. Any man may do a good deed or make a good gift on the spur of the moment, or under the pressure of some superstition or priestcraft; but the real lover of mankind is he who is jealous of none. The so-called great men of the world may all be seen to become jealous of each other for a small name, for a little fame, and for a few bits of gold. So long as this jealousy exists in a heart it is far away from the perfection of *Ahimsâ*, The cow does not eat meat, nor does the sheep. Are they great *Yogins*, great non-injurers (*Ahimsakas*)? Any fool may abstain from eating this or that; surely that gives him no more distinction than to herbivorous animals. The man who will mercilessly cheat widows and orphans, and do the vilest deeds for money, is worse than any brute, even if he lives entirely on grass alone. The man whose heart never cherishes even the thought of injury to anyone, who rejoices at the prosperity of even his greatest enemy, that man is the *Bhakta*, he is the *Yogin*, he is the *Guru* of all, even though he lives every day of his life on the flesh of swine. Therefore, we must always remember that external practices have value only as helps to develop internal purity. It is better to have internal purity alone when minute attention to external observances is not practicable. But woe unto the man and woe unto the nation, that forgets the real, internal, spiritual essentials of religion, and mechanically clutches with death-like grasp all the external forms and never lets them go. The forms have value only so far as they are the expressions of the life within. If they have ceased to express life, crush them out without mercy.

The next means to the attainment of *Bhakti-Yoga* is strength (*anavasâda*). "This *Âtman* is not to be attained by the weak," says the *Śruti*. Both physical weakness and mental weakness are meant here. "The strong, the hardy," are the only fit students. What can puny, little, decrepit things do? They will break to pieces, whenever the mysterious forces of the body and mind are even slightly awakened by the practice of any of the *Yogas*. It is "the young, the healthy, the strong" that can score success. Physical strength, therefore, is absolutely necessary. It is the strong body alone that can bear the shock of re-action resulting from the attempt to control the organs. He who wants to become a *Bhakta* must be strong, must be healthy. When the miserably weak attempt any of the *Yogas*, they are likely to get some incurable malady, or they weaken their minds. Voluntarily weakening the body is really no prescription for spiritual enlightenment.

The mentally weak also cannot succeed in attaining the *Âtman*. The person who aspires to be a *Bhakta* must be cheerful. It is the cheerful mind that is persevering. It is the strong mind that hews its way through a thousand difficulties. And this, the hardest task of all, the cutting of our way out of the net of *Mâyâ*, is the work reserved only for giant wills.

Yet at the same time excessive mirth should be avoided (*anuddharsha*). Excessive mirth makes us unfit for serious thought. It also fritters away the energies of the mind in vain. The stronger the will, the less the yielding to the sway of the emotions. Excessive hilarity is quite as objectionable as too much of sad seriousness, and all religious realisation is possible only when the mind is in a steady, peaceful condition of harmonious equilibrium. It is thus that one may begin to learn how to love the Lord.

PARÂ-BHAKTI-YOGA

SUPREME DEVOTION

I. The Preparatory Renunciation

We have now finished the consideration of what may be called the preparatory *Bhakti* and are entering on the study of the *Parâ-Bhakti,* or supreme devotion. We have to speak of a preparation to the practice of this *Parâ-Bhakti,*. All such preparations are intended only for the purification of the soul. The repetition of names, the rituals, the forms, and the symbols, all these various things are for the purification of the soul. The greatest purifier among all such things, a purifier without which no one enters the regions of this higher devotion (*Parâ-Bhakti,*), is renunciation. It is a frightening thing to many; yet, without it, there cannot be any spiritual growth. In all our *Yoga's* this renunciation is necessary. This is the steppingstone and the real centre and the real heart of all spiritual culture renunciation. This is religion renunciation. When the human soul draws back from the things of the world and tries to go into deeper things; when man, the spirit which is here somewhat being concretised and materialised, understands that he is thereby going to be destroyed and to be reduced almost into mere matter, and turns his face away from matter, then begins renunciation, then begins real spiritual growth. The *Karma-Yogin's* renunciation is in the shape of giving up all the fruits of his actions; he is not attached to the results of his labours; he does not care for any reward here or hereafter. The *Râja-Yogin* knows that the whole of nature is intended for the soul to acquire experience, and that the result of all the experiences of the soul is for it to become aware of its eternal separateness from nature. The human soul has to understand and realize that it has been spirit, and not matter, through eternity; and that this conjunction of it with matter is and can be only for a time. The *Râja-Yogin* learns the lesson of renunciation through his own experience of nature. The *Jnâna-Yogin* has the harshest of all renunciations to go through, as he has to realise from the very first that the whole of this solid-looking nature is all an illusion. He has to understand that all that is any kind of manifestation of power in nature belongs to the soul, and not to nature. He has to know, from the very start, that all knowledge and all experiences are in the soul, and not in nature; so, he has at once and by the sheer force of rational conviction to tear himself off from all bondage to nature. He lets nature and all her things go, he lets them vanish and tries to stand alone!

Of all renunciations, the most natural, so to say, is that of the *Bhakti-Yogin*. Here there is no violence, nothing to give up, nothing to tear off, as it were, from ourselves, nothing from which we have violently to separate ourselves, the *Bhakta's* renunciation is easy, smooth, flowing, and as natural as the things around us. We see the manifestation of this sort of renunciation, although more or less in the shape of caricatures, every day around us. A man begins to love a woman; after a while he loves another, and the first woman he lets go. She drops out of his mind smoothly, gently, without his feeling the want of her at all. A woman loves a man; she then begins to love another man, and the first one drops off from her mind quite naturally. A man loves his own city, then he begins to love his country, and the intense love for his little city drops off smoothly, naturally. Again, a man learns to love the whole world; his love for his country, his intense, fanatical patriotism drops off, without hurting him, without any manifestation of violence. Uncultured man loves the pleasures of the senses intensely; as he becomes cultured, he begins to love intellectual pleasures, and his sense-enjoyments become less and less. No man can enjoy a meal with the same gusto of pleasure as a dog or a wolf, but those pleasures, which a man gets from intellectual experiences and achievements, the dog can never enjoy. At first, pleasure is in association with the lower senses; but as soon as an animal reaches a higher plane of existence, the lower kind of pleasures become less intense. In human society the nearer the man is to the animal, the stronger is his pleasure in the senses; and the higher and the more cultured the man is, the greater is his pleasure in intellectual and such other finer pursuits. So, when a man gets even higher than the plane of the intellect, higher than that of mere thought, when he get to the plane of spirituality and of divine inspiration, he finds there a state of bliss, compared to which all the pleasures of the senses, or even of the intellect, are as nothing. When the moon shines brightly all the stars become dim, and when the sun shines the moon, herself becomes dim. The renunciation necessary for the attainment of *Bhakti* is not obtained by killing anything, but just comes in as naturally as, in the presence of an increasingly stronger light, the less intense ones become dimmer and dimmer until they vanish away completely. So, this love of the pleasures of the senses and of the intellect is all made dim and thrown aside and cast into the shade by the love of God Himself. That love of God grows and assumes a form which is called *Parâ-Bhakti,* or supreme devotion. Forms vanish, rituals fly away, books are superseded, images, temples, churches, religions, and sects, countries and nationalities, all these little limitations and bondages fall off by their own nature from him who knows this love of God. Nothing remains to bind him or fetter his freedom. A ship, all of a sudden, comes near a magnetic rock and its iron bolts and bars are all attracted and drawn out, and the planks get loosened and freely float on the water. Divine grace thus loosens the binding bolts and bars of the soul, and it becomes free. So, in this renunciation auxiliary to devotion, there is no harshness, no dryness, no struggle, no repression or suppression. The *Bhakta* has not to suppress any single one of his emotions, he only strives to intensify them and direct them to God.

II. The Bhakta's Renunciation Results From Love

We see love everywhere in nature. Whatever in society is good and great and sublime, is the working out of that love; whatever in society is very bad, nay diabolical, is also the ill-directed working out of the same emotion of love. It is this same emotion that gives us the pure and holy conjugal love between husband and wife, as well as the sort of love which goes to satisfy the lowest forms of animal passion. The emotion is the same, but its manifestation is different in the different cases. It is the same feeling of love, well or ill-directed, that impels one man to do good and to give all he has to the poor, while it makes another man cut the throats of his brethren and take away all their possessions. The former loves others as much as the latter loves himself. The direction of the love is bad in the case of this latter, but it is right and proper in the other case. The same fire that cooks a meal for us may burn a child, and it is no fault of the fire if it did so; the difference lies in the way in which it is used. Therefore, love, the intense longing for association, the strong desire on the part of two to become one, and, it may be after all, of all to become merged in one, is being manifested everywhere in higher or lower forms as the case may be. *Bhakti-Yoga* is the science of higher love; it shows us how to direct it; it shows us how to control it, how to manage it, how to use it, how to give it a new aim, as it were, and from it obtain the highest and most glorious results, that is, how to make it lead us to spiritual blessedness. Bhakti-Yoga does not say "Give up;" it only says "Love; love the Highest;" and everything low naturally falls off from him the object of whose love is this Highest.

"I cannot tell anything about Thee, except that Thou art my love. Thou art beautiful, Oh Thou art beautiful! Thou art beauty itself." What is after all really required of us in this Yoga is that our thirst after the beautiful should be directed to God. What is the beauty in the human face, in the sky, in the stars, and in the moon? It is only the partial apprehension of the real all-embracing Divine Beauty. "He is shining, everything shines. It is through His light that all things shine." Take this high position of *Bhakti* which makes you forget at once all your little personalities. Take yourself away from all the world's little selfish clinging's. Do not look upon humanity as the centre of all your human and higher interests. Stand as a witness, as a student, and observe the phenomena of nature. Have the feeling of personal non-attachment with regard to man and see how this mighty feeling of love is working itself out in the world. Sometimes a little friction is produced, but that is only in the course of the struggle to attain the higher real love. Sometimes there is a little fight, or a little fall; but it is all only along the way. Stand aside, and freely let these frictions come. You feel the frictions only when you are in the current of the world, but when you are outside of it simply as a witness and as a student, you will be able to see that there are millions and millions of channels in which God is manifesting Himself as Love.

"Wherever there is any bliss, even though in the most sensual of things, there is a spark of that Eternal Bliss which is the Lord Himself." Even in the lowest kinds of attraction there is the germ of Divine love. One of the names of the Lord in Sanskrit is *Hari*, and this means that He attracts all things to Himself. His is in fact the only attraction worthy of human hearts. Who can attract a soul really? Only He! Do you think dead matter can truly attract the soul? It never did, and never will. When you see a man going after a beautiful face, do you think that it is the handful of arranged material molecules which really attracts the man? Not at all. Behind those material particles there must be and is the play of divine influence and divine love. The ignorant man does not know it; but yet, consciously or unconsciously, he is attracted by it and it alone. So even the lowest forms of attraction derive their power from God Himself. "None, O beloved, ever loved the husband for the husband's sake; it is the *Âtman*, the Lord, who is inside, and for His sake the husband is loved." Loving wives may know this, or they may not; it is true all the same "None, O beloved, ever loved the wife for the wife's sake, but it is the Self within the wife that is loved." Similarly, no one loves a child or anything else in the world except on account of Him who is within. The Lord is the great magnet, and we are all like iron filings; all of us are being constantly attracted by Him, and all of us are struggling to reach Him. All this struggling of ours in this world is surely not intended for selfish ends. Fools do not know what they are doing; the work of their life is all to approach the great magnet. All the tremendous struggling and fighting in life is intended to make us go to Him ultimately and be one with Him.

However, the *Bhakti-Yogin* knows the meaning of life's struggles; he understands it. He has passed through a long series of these struggles, and knows what they mean, and earnestly desires to be free from the friction thereof; he wants to avoid the clash and go direct to the centre of all attractions, the great *Hari*. This is the renunciation of the *Bhakta*; this mighty attraction, in the direction of God makes all other attractions vanish for him; this mighty infinite love of God which enters his heart leaves no place for any other love to live there. How can it be otherwise? *Bhakti* fills his heart with the divine waters of the ocean of love, which is God Himself; there is no place there for little loves. That is to say, the *Bhakta's* renunciation is that vairâgya, or non-attachment for all things that are not God, which results from *anurâga*, or great attachment to God.

This is the ideal preparation for the attainment of the supreme *Bhakti*. When this renunciation comes, the gate opens for the soul to pass through and reach the lofty regions of Supreme Devotion or *Parâ-Bhakti*. Then it is that we begin to understand what *Parâ-Bhakti* is; and the man who has entered into the inner shrine of the *Parâ-Bhakti*, he alone has the right to say that all forms and symbols are useless to him as aids to religious realisation. He alone has attained that supreme state of love commonly called the brotherhood of man; the rest only talk. He sees no distinctions; the mighty ocean of love has entered into him, and he sees not man in man, but beholds his Beloved everywhere. Through every face shines to him his *Hari*. The light in the sun or the moon is all His manifestation. Wherever there is beauty or sublimity, to him it is all His. Such *Bhaktas* are still living; the world is never without them. Such, though bitten by a serpent, only say that a messenger came for them from their Beloved. Such men alone have the right to talk of universal brotherhood. They feel no resentment; their minds never react in the form of hatred, or of jealousy. The external, the sensuous, has vanished from them forever. How can they be angry, when, through their love, they are always able to see the Reality behind the scenes?

III. The Naturalness Of Bhakti-Yoga And Its Central Secret

"Those who with constant attention always worship You, and those who worship the Undifferentiated, the Absolute, of these who are the greater *Yogins*?" Arjuna asked of Sri Krishna. The answer was: "Those who concentrating their minds on Me worship Me with eternal constancy and are endowed with the highest faith they are My best worshippers; they are the greatest *Yogins*. Those that worship the Absolute, the Indescribable, the Undifferentiated, the Omnipresent, the Unthinkable, the All-comprehending, the Immovable, and the Eternal, by controlling the play of their organs and having the conviction of sameness in regard to all things, they also, being engaged in doing good to all beings, come to Me alone. But to those whose minds have been devoted to the unmanifested Absolute, the difficulty of the struggle along the way is much greater, for it is indeed with great difficulty that the path of the unmanifested Absolute is trodden by any embodied being. Those who, having offered up all their work unto Me, with entire reliance in Me, meditate on Me and worship Me without any attachment to anything else them I soon lift up from the ocean of death and ever-recurring birth, as their mind is wholly attached to Me." *Jnâna-Yoga* and *Bhakti-Yoga* are both referred to here. Both may be said to have been defined in the above passage. *Jnâna-Yoga* is grand; it is high philosophy; and almost every human being thinks, curiously enough, that he can surely do everything required of him by philosophy; but it is really very difficult to live truly the life of philosophy. We are often apt to run into great dangers in trying to guide our life by philosophy. This world may be said to be divided between persons of demoniacal nature, who think the care-taking of the body to be the be-all and the end-all of existence, and persons of godly nature who realise that the body is simply a means to an end, an instrument intended for the culture of the soul. The devil can and indeed does quote the scriptures for its own purposes; and thus, the way of knowledge appears to offer justification to what the bad man does as much as it offers inducements to what the good man does. This is the great danger in *Jnâna-Yoga*. But *Bhakti-Yoga* is natural, sweet, and gentle; the *Bhakta* does not take such high flights as the *Jnâna-Yogin*, and therefore he is not apt to have such big falls. Until the bond ages of the soul pass away, it cannot of course be free, whatever may be the nature of the path that the religious man takes.

Here is a passage showing how, in the case of one of the blessed *Gopîs,* the soul-binding chains of both merit and demerit were broken. "The intense pleasure in meditating on God took away the binding effects of her good deeds. Then her intense misery of soul in not attaining unto Him washed off all her sinful propensities, and she became free." In *Bhakti-Yoga* the central secret is, therefore, to know that the various passions and feelings and emotions in the human heart are not wrong in themselves; only they have to be carefully controlled and given a higher and higher direction, until they attain the very highest condition of excellence. The highest direction is that which takes us to God; every other direction is lower. We find that pleasure and pain are very common and oft-recurring feelings in our lives. When a man feels pain, because he has not got wealth or some such worldly thing, he is giving a wrong direction to the feeling. Still pain has its uses. Let a man feel pain that he has not reached the Highest, that he has not reached God, and that pain will be to his salvation. When you become glad that you have got a handful of coins, it is a wrong direction given to the faculty of joy; it should be given a higher direction, it must be made to serve the Highest Ideal. Pleasure in that kind of ideal must surely be our highest joy. This same thing is true of all our other feelings. The Bhakta says that not one of them is wrong, he gets hold of them all and points them unfailingly towards God.

IV. The Forms Of Love-Manifestation

Here are some of the forms in which love manifests itself. First there is reverence. Why do people show reverence to temples and holy places? Because He is worshipped there, and His presence is associated with all such places. Why do people in every country pay reverence to teachers of religion? It is natural for the human heart to do so, because all such teachers preach the Lord. At bottom, reverence is a growth out of love; we can none of us revere him whom we do not love. Then comes *Prîti* pleasure in God. What an immense pleasure men take in the objects of their senses! They go anywhere, run through any danger, to get the thing which they love, the thing which their senses like. What is wanted of the *Bhakta* is this very kind of intense love which has, however, to be directed to God. Then there is the sweetest of pains, *Viraha*, the intense misery due to the absence of the beloved. When a man feels intense misery, because he has not attained to God, has not known that which is the only thing worthy to be known, and becomes in consequence very dissatisfied and almost mad then there is *Viraha* and this state of the mind makes it feel disturbed in the presence of anything other than the beloved. In earthly love we see how often this

Viraha comes. Again, when men are really and intensely in love with women, or women with men, they feel a kind of natural annoyance in the presence of all those whom they do not love. Exactly the same state of impatience, in regard to things that are not loved, comes to the mind, when *Parâ-Bhakti* holds sway over it; even to talk about things other than God becomes distasteful then. "Think of Him, think of Him alone, and give up all other vain words." Those who talk of Him alone, the *Bhakta* finds to be friendly to him; while those who talk of anything else appear to him to be unfriendly. A still higher stage of love is reached when life itself is maintained for the sake of the one Ideal of Love, when life itself is considered beautiful and worth living only on account of that Love. Without it, such a life would not remain even for a moment. Life is sweet because it thinks of the Beloved. *Tadîyatâ (Hisness)* comes when a man becomes perfect according to *Bhakti*; when he has become blessed, when he has attained to God, when he has touched the feet of God, as it were, his whole nature is purified and completely changed. All his purposes in life then become fulfilled. Yet, many such *Bhaktas* live on just to worship Him. That is the bliss, the only pleasure in life, which they will not give up. "Oh king, such is the blessed quality of *Hari* that even those, who have become satisfied with everything, all the knots of whose hearts have been cut asunder, even they love the Lord for love's sake" the Lord "whom all the gods worship, all the lovers of liberation, and all the knowers of the *Brahman*." Such is the power of love. When a man has forgotten himself altogether, and does not feel that anything belongs to him, then he acquires the state of *Tadîyatâ*; everything is sacred to him, because it belongs to the Beloved. Even in regard to earthly love the lover thinks that everything belonging to his beloved is so sacred and so dear to him. He loves even a bit of the cloth belonging to the darling of his heart. In the same way, when a person loves the Lord, the whole universe becomes so dear to him, because it is all His.

V. Universal Love And How It Leads To Self-Surrender

How can we love the *vyashti*, the particular, without first loving the *samashti*, the universal? God is the *samashti*, the generalised and the abstract universal whole; and the universe that we see is the *vyashti*, the particularised thing. To love the whole universe is possible only by way of loving the *samashti* the universal which is, as it were, the one unity in which are to be found millions and millions of smaller unities. The philosophers of India do not stop at the particulars; they cast a hurried glance at the particulars, and immediately start to find the generalised forms which will include all the particulars. The search after the universal is the one search of Indian philosophy and religion. The *Jnânin* aims at the wholeness of things, at that one absolute and generalised Being, knowing which, he knows everything. The *Bhakta* wishes to realise that one generalised abstract Person, in loving Whom, he loves the whole universe. The *Yogin* wishes to have possession of that one generalised form of power, by controlling which he controls his whole universe. The Indian mind, throughout its history, has been directed to this kind of singular search after the universal in everything in science, in psychology, in love, in philosophy. So, the conclusion to which the *Bhakta* comes is that, if you go on merely loving one person after another, you may go on loving them so for an infinite length of time without being in the least able to love the world as a whole. When, at last, the central idea is, however, arrived at, that the sum-total of all love is God, that the sum-total of the aspirations of all the souls in the universe, whether they be free, or bound, or struggling towards liberation, is God, then alone it becomes possible for anyone to put forth universal love. God is the *samashti*, and this visible universe is God differentiated and made manifest. If we love this sum-total, we love everything. Loving the world and doing it good will all come easily then; we have to obtain this power only by loving God first; otherwise, it is no joke to do good to the world. "Everything is His and He is my Lover; I love Him," says the *Bhakta*. In this way everything becomes sacred to the Bhakta, because all things are His. All are His children, His body, His manifestation. How then may we hurt anyone? How then may we not love anyone? With the love of God will come, as a sure effect, the love of everyone in the universe. The nearer we approach to God, the more do we begin to see that all things are in Him. When the soul succeeds in appropriating the bliss of this supreme love, it also begins to see Him in everything. Our heart will thus become an eternal fountain of love. And when we reach even higher states of this love, all the little differences between the things of the world are entirely lost; man is seen no more as man, but only as God; the animal is seen no more as animal, but as God; even the tiger is no more a tiger, but a manifestation of God. Thus, in this intense state of *Bhakti*, worship is offered to everyone, to every life, and to every being. "Knowing that Hari, the Lord, is in every being, the wise have thus to manifest unswerving love towards all beings." As a result of this kind of intense all-absorbing love, comes the feeling of perfect self-surrender, the conviction that nothing that happens is against us. Then the loving soul is able to say, if pain comes, "Welcome pain." If misery comes, it will say "Welcome misery, you are also from the Beloved." If a serpent comes, it will say "Welcome serpent." If death comes, such a *Bhakta* will welcome it with a smile. "Blessed am I that they all come to me; they are all welcome." The *Bhakta* in this state of perfect resignation, arising out of intense love to God and to all that are His, ceases to distinguish between pleasure and pain in so far as they affect him. He does not know what it is to complain of pain or misery; and this kind of uncomplaining resignation to the will of God, who is all love, is indeed a worthier acquisition than all the glory of grand and heroic performances.

To the vast majority of mankind, the body is everything; the body is all the universe to them; bodily enjoyment is their all in all. This demon of the worship of the body and of the things of the body has entered into us all. We may indulge in tall talk, and take very high flights, but we are like vultures all the same; our mind is directed to the piece of carrion down below. Why should our body be saved, say, from the tiger? Why may we not give it over to the tiger? The tiger will thereby be pleased, and that is not altogether so very far from self-sacrifice and worship. Can you reach the realisation of such an idea in which all sense of self is completely lost? It is a very dizzy height on the pinnacle of the religion of love, and few in this world have ever climbed up to it; but until a man reaches that highest point of ever-ready and ever-willing self-sacrifice he cannot become a perfect *Bhakta*. We may all manage to maintain our bodies more or less satisfactorily and for longer or shorter intervals of time. Nevertheless, our bodies have to go; there is no permanence about them. Blessed are they whose bodies get destroyed in the service of others. "Wealth, and even life itself, the sage always holds ready for the service of others. In this world, there being one thing certain, *viz.*, death, it is far better that this body dies in a good cause than in a bad one." We may drag our life on for fifty years or a hundred years; but after that, what is it that happens? Everything that is the result of combination must get dissolved and die. There must and will come a time for it to be decomposed. Jesus and Buddha and Mohammed are all dead; all the great prophets and teachers of the world are dead. "In this evanescent world, where everything is falling to pieces, we have to make the highest use of what time we have," says the *Bhakta*; and really the highest use of life is to hold it at the service of all beings. It is the horrible body-idea that breeds all the selfishness in the world, just this one delusion that we are wholly the body we own, and that we must by all possible means try our very best to preserve and to please it. If you know that you are positively other than your body, you have then none to fight with or struggle against; you are dead to all ideas of selfishness. So, the *Bhakta* declares that we have to hold ourselves as if we are altogether dead to all things of the world; and that is indeed self-surrender. Let things come as they may. This is the meaning of "Thy will be done;" not going about fighting and struggling and thinking all the while that God wills all our own weaknesses and worldly ambitions. It may be that good comes even out of our selfish struggles; that is, however, God's look out. The perfected *Bhakta's* idea must be never to will and work for himself. "Lord, they build high temples in Your name; they make large gifts in Your name; I am poor; I am nothing; so, I take this body of mine and place it at Your feet. Do not give me up, O Lord." Such is the prayer proceeding out of the depths of the *Bhakta's* heart. To him who has experienced it, this eternal sacrifice of the self-unto the Beloved Lord is higher by far than all wealth and power, than even all soaring thoughts of renown and enjoyment. The peace of the *Bhakta's* calm resignation is a peace that passed all understanding and is of incomparable value. His *Aprâtikûlya* is a state of the mind in which it has no interests, and naturally knows nothing that is opposed to them. In this state of sublime resignation everything in the shape of attachment goes away completely, except that one all-absorbing love to Him in Whom all things live and move and have their being. This attachment of love to God is, indeed, one that does not bind the soul but effectively breaks all its bondages.

VI. The Higher Knowledge And The Higher Love Are One To The True Lover

The *Upanishads* distinguish between higher knowledge and a lower knowledge; and to the *Bhakta* there is really no difference between this higher knowledge and this higher love (Para-*bhakti*). The *Mundaka Upanishad* says: "The knowers of the *Brahman* declare that there are two kinds of knowledge worthy to be known, namely, the Higher (*Parâ*) and the Lower (*Aparâ*). Of these the Lower (knowledge) consists of the *Rigveda*, the *Yajurveda*, the *Sâmaveda* the *Atharvaveda*, the *Śîkshâ* (or the science dealing with pronunciation and accent), the *Kalpa* (or the sacrificial liturgy), Grammar, the *Nirukta* (or the science dealing with etymology and the meaning of words), Prosody, and Astronomy; and the Higher (knowledge) is that by which that Unchangeable is known." The higher knowledge is thus clearly shown to be the knowledge of the *Brahman*; and the *Devî-Bhâgavata* gives us the following definition of the higher love (*Parâ-bhakti*): "As oil poured from one vessel to another falls in an unbroken line, so, when the mind in an unbroken stream thinks of the Lord, we have what is called *Parâ-bhakti* or supreme love." This kind of undisturbed and ever steady direction of the mind and the heart to the Lord with an inseparable attachment is indeed the highest manifestation of man's love to God. All other forms of *Bhakti* are only preparatory for the attainment of this highest form thereof, *viz.*, the *Parâ-Bhakti* which is also known as the love that comes after attachment (*Râgânugâ*). When this supreme love once comes into the heart of man, his mind will continuously think of God and remember nothing else. He will give no room in himself to thoughts other than those of God, and his soul will be unconquerably pure, and will alone break all the bonds of mind and matter and become serenely free. He alone can worship the Lord in his own heart; to him forms, symbols, books and doctrines are all unnecessary and are incapable of proving serviceable in any way. It is not easy to love the Lord thus. Ordinarily human love is seen to flourish only in places where it is returned; where love is not returned for love, cold indifference is the natural result. There are, however, rare instances in which we may notice love exhibiting itself even where there is no return of love. We may compare this kind of love, for purposes of illustration, to the love of the moth for the fire; the insect loves the fire, falls into it and dies. It is indeed in the nature of this insect to love so. To love, because it is the nature of love to love, is undeniably the highest and most unselfish manifestation of love that may be seen in the world. Such love working itself out on the plane of spirituality necessarily leads to the attainment of *Parâ-bhakti*.

VII. The Triangle Of Love

We may represent love as a triangle, each of the angles of which corresponds to one of its inseparable characteristics. There can be no triangle without all its three angles; and there can be no true love without its three following characteristics. The first angle of our triangle of love is that love knows no bargaining. Wherever there is any seeking for something in return, there can be no real love; it becomes a mere matter of shop-keeping. As long as there is in us any idea of deriving this or that favour from God in return for our respect and allegiance to Him, so long there can be no true love growing in our hearts. Those who worship God because they wish Him to bestow favours on them are sure not to worship Him if those favours are not forthcoming. The *Bhakta* loves the Lord because He is lovable; there is no other motive originating or directing this divine emotion of the true devotee. We have heard it said that a great king once went into a forest and there met a sage. He talked with the sage a little and was very much pleased with his purity and wisdom. The king then wanted the sage to oblige him by receiving a present from him. The sage refused to do so, saying, "The fruits of the forest are food enough for me; the pure streams of water flowing downb from the mountains give enough of drink for me; the barks of the trees supply me with enough of covering; and the caves of the mountains form my home. Why should I take any present from you or from anybody?" The king said, "Just to benefit me, sir, please take something from my hands, and please go with me to the city and to my palace." After much persuasion, the sage at last consented to do as the king desired and went with him to his palace. Before offering the gift to the sage the king repeated his prayers, saying, "Lord, give me more children; Lord, give me more wealth; Lord, give me more territory; Lord, keep my body in better health;" and so on. Before the king finished saying his prayer the sage had got up and walked away from the room quietly. At seeing this the king became perplexed and began to follow him, crying aloud, "Sir, you are going away, you have not taken my presents." The sage turned round and said, "Beggar, I do not beg of beggars. You are a beggar yourself, and how can you give me anything? I am no fool to think of taking anything from a beggar like you. Go away, do not follow me." There is well brought out the distinction between mere beggars and the real lovers of God. To worship God even for the sake of salvation or any other reward is equally degenerate. Love knows no reward. Love is always for love's sake. The *Bhakta* loves because he cannot help loving. When you see beautiful scenery and fall in love with it, you do not demand anything in the way of favour from the scenery; nor does the scenery demand anything from you. Yet the vision thereof brings you to a blissful state of the mind, it tones down all the friction in your soul, it makes you calm, almost raises you, for the time being, beyond your mortal nature, and places you in a condition of quite divine ecstasy; this nature of real love is the first angle of our triangle. Ask not anything in return for your love; let your position be always that of the giver; give your love unto God, but do not ask anything in return even from Him.

The second angle of the triangle of love is that love knows no fear. Those that love God through fear are the lowest of human beings, quite undeveloped as men. They worship God from fear of punishment. He is a great Being to them, with a whip in one hand and the sceptre in the other; if they do not obey Him, they are afraid they will be whipped. It is a degradation to worship God through fear of punishment; such worship is, if worship at all, the crudest form of the worship of love. So long as there is any fear in the heart, how can there be love also? Love conquers naturally all fear. Think of a young mother in the street, and if a dog barks at her she is frightened; she flies into the nearest house. Suppose the same mother is in the street with her child, and a lion springs upon the child. Where then will the mother's place be? Of course, at the mouth of the lion. Love does conquer all fear. Fear comes from the selfish idea of cutting one's self off from the universe. The smaller and the more selfish I make myself, the more is my fear. If a man thinks he is a little nothing, fear will surely come upon him. And the less you think of yourself as an insignificant person, the less fear will there be for you. So long as there is the least spark of fear in you there can be no love there. Love and fear are incompatible; God is never to be feared by those who love Him. The commandment, "Do not take the name of the Lord thy God in vain," the true lover of God laughs at. How can there be any blasphemy in the religion of love? The more you take the name of the Lord, the better for you, in whatever way you may do it. You are only repeating His name because you love Him.

The third angle of the love-triangle is that love knows no rival, for in it is always embodied the lover's highest ideal. True love never comes until the object of our love becomes to us our highest ideal. It may be that in many cases human love is misdirected and misplaced, but to the person who loves, the thing he loves is always his own highest ideal. One may see his ideal in the vilest of beings, and another in the highest of beings; nevertheless, in every case it is the ideal alone that can be truly and intensely loved. The highest ideal of every man is called God. Ignorant or wise, saint or sinner, man or woman, educated or uneducated, cultivated or uncultivated, to every human being the highest ideal is God. The synthesis of all the highest ideals of beauty, of sublimity, and of power gives us the completest conception of the loving and lovable God. These ideals exist, in some shape or other, in every mind naturally; they form a part and parcel of all our minds. All the active manifestations of human nature are struggles of those ideals to become realised in practical life. All the various movements that we see around us in society are caused by the various ideals in various souls trying to come out and become concretised; what is inside presses on to come outside. This perennially dominant influence of the ideal is the one force, the one motive power, that may be seen to be constantly working in the midst of mankind. It may be after hundreds of births, after struggling through thousands of years, that man finds out that it is vain to try to make the inner ideal mould completely the external conditions and square well with them; after realising this he no more tries to project his own ideal on the outside world, but worships the ideal itself as ideal, from the highest standpoint of love. This ideally perfect ideal embraces all lower ideals. Everyone admits the truth of the saying that a lover sees Helen's beauty on an Ethiop's brow. The man who is standing aside as a looker-on sees that love is here misplaced, but the lover sees his Helen all the same, and does not see the Ethiop at all. Helen or Ethiop, the objects of our love are really the centres round which our ideals become crystallised. What is it that the world commonly worships? Not certainly this all-embracing ideally perfect ideal of the supreme devotee and lover. That ideal which men and woman commonly worship is what is in themselves; every person projects his or her own ideal on the outside world and kneels before it. That is why we find that men who are cruel and bloodthirsty conceive of a blood-thirsty God, because they can only love their own highest ideal. That is why good men have a very high ideal of God; and their ideal is indeed so very different from that of others.

VIII. The God Of Love Is His Own Proof

What is the ideal of the lover who has quite passed beyond the idea of selfishness, of bartering and bargaining, and who knows no fear? Even to the great God such a man will say "I will give you my all, and I do not want anything from you; indeed, there is nothing that I can call my own." When a man has acquired this conviction, his ideal becomes one of perfect love, one of the perfect fearlessness of love. The highest ideal of such a person has no narrowness of particularity about it; it is love universal, love without limits and bounds, love itself, absolute love. This grand ideal of the religion of love is worshipped and loved absolutely as such without the aid of any symbols or suggestions. This is the highest form of *Parâ-bhakti*, the worship of such an all-comprehending ideal as the ideal; all the other forms of *Bhakti* are only stages on the way to reach it. All our failures and all our successes in following the religion of love are on the road to the realisation of that one ideal. Object after object is taken up, and the inner ideal is successively projected on it all; and all such external objects are found inadequate as exponents of the ever-expanding inner ideal, and are naturally rejected one after another. At last, the aspirant begins to think that it is vain to try to realise the ideal in external objects, that all external objects are as nothing when compared with the ideal itself; and, in course of time, he acquires the power of realising the highest and the most generalised abstract ideal entirely as an abstraction that is to him quite alive and real. When the devotee has reached this point, he is no more impelled to ask whether God can be demonstrated or not, whether He is omnipotent and omniscient, or not. To him He is only the God of Love; He is the highest ideal of love and that is sufficient for all his purposes; He, as love, is self-evident; it requires no proofs to demonstrate the existence of the beloved to the lover. The magistrate-gods of other forms of religion may require a good deal of proof to prove them, but the *Bhakta* does not and cannot think of such gods at all. To him God exists entirely as Love. "None, O beloved, loves the husband for the husband's sake, but it is for the sake of the Self who is in the husband that the husband is loved; none, O beloved, loves the wife for the wife's sake, but it is for the sake of the Self who is in the wife that the wife is loved." It is said by some that selfishness is the only motive power in regard to all human activities. That also is love lowered by being particularised. When I think of myself as comprehending the universal, there can surely be no selfishness in me; but when I, by mistake, think that I am a little something, my love becomes particularised and narrowed. The mistake consists in making the sphere of love narrow and contracted. All things in the universe are of divine origin and deserve to be loved; it has, however, to be borne in mind that the love of the whole includes the love of the parts. This whole is the God of the *Bhaktas*, and all the other Gods, Fathers in Heaven, or Rulers, or Creators, and all theories and doctrines and books have no purpose and no meaning for them, seeing that they have through their supreme love and devotion risen above those things altogether. When the heart is purified and cleansed and filled to the brim with the divine nectar of love, all other ideas of God become simply puerile and are rejected as being inadequate or unworthy. Such is indeed the power of *Parâ-Bhakti* or Supreme Love; and the perfected *Bhakta* no more goes to see God in temples and churches; he knows nowhere to go where he will not find Him. He finds Him in the temple as well as out of the temple; he finds Him in the saint's saintliness as well as in the wicked man's wickedness, because he has Him already seated in glory in his own heart, as the one almighty, inextinguishable Light of Love which is ever shining and eternally present.

IX. Human Representations Of The Divine Ideal Of Love

It is impossible to express the nature of this supreme and absolute ideal of love in human language. Even the highest flight of human imagination is incapable of comprehending it in all its infinite perfection and beauty. Nevertheless, the followers of the religion of love in its higher as well as its lower forms have all along and in all countries had to use the inadequate human language to comprehend and to define their own ideal of love. Nay more; human love itself, in all its varied forms, has been made to typify this inexpressible divine love. Man can think of divine things only in his own human way; to us the Absolute can be expressed only in our relative language. The whole universe is to us a writing of the infinite in the language of the finite. Therefore, Bhaktas make use of all the common terms associated with the common love of humanity in relation to God and His worship of love. Some of the great writers on *Parâ-bhakti* have tried to understand and experience this divine love in so many different ways. The lowest form in which this love is apprehended is what they call the peaceful, the *Śânta*. When a man worships God without the fire of love in him, without its madness in his brain, when his love is just the calm commonplace love, a little higher than mere forms and ceremonies and symbols, but not at all characterised by the madness of intensely active love, it is said to be *Śânta*. We see some people in the world who like to move on slowly, and others who come and go like the whirlwind. The *Śânta-Bhakta* is calm, peaceful, gentle. The next higher type is that of *Dâsya* (servantship); it comes when a man thinks he is the servant of the Lord. The attachment of the faithful servant unto the master is his ideal. The next is what is known as *Vâtsalya*, loving God not as our Father but as our Child. This may look peculiar, but it is a discipline to enable us to detach all ideas of power from the concept of God. The idea of power brings with it awe. There should be no awe in love. The ideas of reverence and obedience are necessary for the formation of character, but when character is formed, when the lover has tasted the calm, peaceful love, and tasted also a little of its intense madness, then he need talk no more of ethics and discipline. To conceive God as mighty, majestic and glorious, as the Lord of the Universe, or as the God of Gods, the lover says he does not care. It is to avoid this association with God of the fear-creating sense of power that he worships God as his own child. The mother and the father are not moved by awe in relation to the child; they cannot have any reverence for the child. They cannot think of asking any favour from the child. The child's position is always that of the receiver, and out of love for the child the parents will give up their bodies a hundred times over. A thousand lives they will sacrifice for that one child of theirs, and therefore God is loved as a child. This idea of loving God as a child comes into existence and grows naturally among those religious sects which believe in the incarnation of God. To the Mahomedans it is impossible to have this idea of God as a child; they will shrink from it with a kind of horror. But the Christian and the Hindu can realise it easily, because they have the baby Jesus and the baby Krishna. The women in India often look upon themselves as Krishna's mothers, Christian mothers also may take up the idea that they are all Christ's mothers, and it will bring to the West the knowledge of God's Divine Motherhood which they so much need. The superstitions of awe and reverence in relation to God are deeply rooted in the heart of our hearts, and it takes long years entirely to sink in love our ideas of reverence and veneration, of awe and majesty and glory with regard to God.

The next type of love is *Sakhya* (friendship). "Thou art our beloved friend." Just as a man opens his heart to his friend and knows that the friend will never chide him for his faults, but will always try to help him, just as there is the idea of equality between him and his friend, so equal love flows in and out between the worshipper and his friendly God. Thus, God becomes our friend, the friend who is near, the friend to whom we may freely tell all the tales of our lives; the innermost secrets of our hearts we may place before him with the greatest assurance of safety and support; He is the friend whom the devotee accepts as an equal; God is viewed here as our playmate. We may well say that we are all playing in this universe. Just as children play their games, just as the most glorious kings and emperors play their own games, so is the Beloved Lord Himself in sport with this universe. He is perfect; He does not want anything. Why should He create? Activity is always with us for the fulfilment of a certain want and want always presupposes imperfection. God is perfect; He has no wants. Why should He go on with this work of an ever-active creation? What purpose has He in view? The stories about God creating this world, for some end or other that we imagine, are good as stories, but not otherwise. It is all really in sport; the universe is His play going on. The whole universe must after all be a big piece of pleasing fun to Him. If you are poor enjoy that as a fun; if you are rich enjoy the fun of being rich; if dangers, come, it is also good fun; if happiness comes there is more good fun. The world is just a play-ground, and we are here having good fun, having a game, and God is with us playing all the while, and we are with Him playing. God is our eternal playmate. How beautifully He is playing! The play is finished, the cycle comes to an end. There is rest for a shorter or longer time, again all come out and play. It is only when you forget that it is all play, and that you are also helping in the play, it is only then that misery and sorrows come; then the heart becomes heavy, then the world weighs upon you with tremendous power; but as soon as you give up the serious idea of reality as the characteristic of the changing incidents of the three minutes of life, and know it to be but a stage on which we are playing, helping Him to play, at once misery ceases for you. He plays in every atom; He is playing when He is building up earths, and suns, and moons; He is playing with the human heart, with animals, with plants. We are his chessmen; He puts the chessmen on the board and shakes them up. He arranges us first in one way and then in another, and we are consciously or unconsciously helping in His play. And Oh bliss! we are His playmates!

There is one more human representation of the divine ideal of love. It is known as *Madhura* (sweet) and is the highest of all such representations. It is indeed based on the highest manifestation of love in this world, and this love is also the strongest known to man. What love shakes the whole nature of man, what love runs through every atom of his being, makes him mad, makes him forget his own nature, transforms him, makes him either a God or a demon as the love between man and woman? In this sweet representation of divine love God is our husband. We are all women; there are no men in this world; there is but the One Man, and that is He, our Beloved. All that love which man gives to woman, or woman to man, has here to be given up to the Lord. All the different kinds of love which we see in the world, and with which we are more or less playing merely, have God as the one goal; only unfortunately man does not know the infinite ocean into which this mighty river of love is constantly flowing;

and so, foolishly, he often tries to direct it to little dolls of human beings. The tremendous love for the child that is in human nature is not for the little doll of a child; if you bestow it blindly and exclusively on the child, you will suffer in consequence; but through such suffering will come the awakening by which you are sure to find out that the love which is in you, if it is given to any human being, will sooner or later bring pain and sorrow as the result. Our love must therefore be given to the Highest One, who never dies and never changes, to Him in the ocean of whose love there is neither ebb nor flow. Love must get to its right destination; it must go unto Him who is really the infinite ocean of love. All rivers flow into the ocean. Even the drop of water coming down from the mountain side cannot stop its course after reaching a brook or a river, however big it may be; at last, even that drop somehow does find its way to the ocean. God is the one goal of all our passions and emotions. If you want to be angry, be angry with Him. Chide your Beloved, chide your Friend. Whom else can you safely chide? Mortal man will not patiently put up with your anger; there will be a reaction. If you are angry with me, I am sure quickly to react, because I cannot patiently put up with your anger. Say unto the Beloved, "Why do You not come to me; why do You leave me thus alone?" Where is there any enjoyment but in Him? What enjoyment can there be in little clods of earth? It is the crystallised essence of infinite enjoyment that we have to seek, and that is in God. Let all our passions and emotions go up unto Him. They are meant for Him, for if they miss their mark and go lower, they become vile; and when they go straight to the mark, the Lord, even the lowest of them becomes transfigured; all the energies of the human body and mind, howsoever they may express themselves, have the Lord as their one goal, as their *Ekâyana*. All loves and all passions of the human heart must go to God. He is the Beloved; whom else can this heart love? He is the most beautiful, the most sublime, He is beauty itself; sublimity itself. Who in this universe is more beautiful than He? Who in this universe is more fit to become the husband than He? Who in this universe is fitter to be loved than He? So let Him be the husband, let Him be the Beloved. Often it so happens that divine lovers who sing of this divine love accept the language of human love in all its aspects as adequate to describe it. Fools do not understand this; they never will. They look at it only with the physical eye. They do not understand the mad throes of this spiritual love. How can they? "One kiss of Thy lips, O Beloved! He that has been kissed by Thee, his thirst for Thee goes on increasing for ever, all his sorrows vanish, and he forgets all things except Thee." Aspire after that kiss of the Beloved, that touch of His lips which makes the *Bhakta* mad, which makes of man a god. To him, who has been blessed with such a kiss, the whole of nature changes, worlds vanish, suns and moons die out and the universe itself melts away into that one infinite ocean of love. That is the perfection of the madness of love. Aye, the true spiritual lover does not rest even there; even the love of husband and wife is not mad enough for him. The *Bhaktas* take up also the idea of illegitimate love, because it is so strong; the impropriety of it is not at all the thing they have in view. The nature of this love is such that the more obstructions there are for its free play the more passionate it becomes. The love between husband and wife is smooth, there are no obstructions there. So, the *Bhaktas* take up the idea of a girl who is in love with her own beloved man, and her mother or father or husband, objects to such love; the more anybody obstructs the course of her love the more is her love tending to grow in strength. Human language cannot describe how Krishna was in the groves of Brinda, how madly he was loved, how at the sound of his voice all rushed out to meet him, the ever-blessed *Gopîs*, forgetting everything, forgetting this world and its ties, its duties, its joy and its sorrows. Man, oh man, you speak of divine love and at the same time are able to attend to all the vanities of this world are you sincere? "Where Râma is, there is no room for any desire where desire is there is no room for Râma: these never coexist like light and darkness they are never together."

X. Conclusion

When this highest ideal of love is reached philosophy is thrown away; who will then care for it? Freedom, Salvation, *Nirvâna* all are thrown away; who cares to become free while in the enjoyment of divine love? "Lord, I do not want wealth, nor friends, nor beauty, nor learning, nor even freedom; let me be born again and again and be Thou ever my Love." Be Thou ever and ever my Love. "Who cares to become sugar," says the *Bhakta*, "I want to taste sugar." Who will then desire to become free and one with God? "I may know that I am He, yet will I take myself away from Him and become different, so that I may enjoy the Beloved." That is what the *Bhakta* says. Love for love's sake is his highest enjoyment. Who will not be bound hand and foot a thousand times over to enjoy the Beloved? No *Bhakta* cares for anything except love, except to love and be loved. His unworldly love is like the tide rushing up the river; this lover goes up the river, against the current. The world calls him mad. I know one whom the world used to call mad, and this was his answer. "My friends, the whole world is a lunatic asylum; some are mad after worldly love, some after name, some after fame, some after money, some after salvation and going to heaven. In this big lunatic asylum, I am also mad, I am mad after God. If you are mad after money, I am mad after God. You are mad; so am

I. I think my madness is after all the best." The true *Bhakta's* love is this burning madness, before which everything else vanishes for him. The whole universe is to him full of love and love alone; that is how it seems to the lover. So, when a man has this love in him, he becomes eternally blessed, eternally happy; this blessed madness of divine love alone can cure for ever the disease of the world that is in us.

We all have to begin as dualists in the religion of love. God is to us a separate being, and we feel ourselves to be separate beings also. Love then comes in the middle, and man begins to approach God, and God also comes nearer and nearer to man. Man takes up all the various relationships of life, as father, as mother, as son, as friend, as master, as lover; and projects them on his ideal of love, on his God. To him God exists as all these, and the last point of his progress is reached when he feels that he has become absolutely merged in the object of his worship. We all begin with love for ourselves, and the unfair claims of the little self-make even love selfish; at last, however, comes the full blaze of light in which this little self is seen to have become one with the one Infinite. Man, himself is so transfigured in the presence of this Light of Love. His heart is cleansed of all impurities and vain desires of which it was more or less full before; and he realises at last the beautiful and inspiring truth that Love, Lover and the Beloved are one.

LIST OF TITLES WITH ISBN NO.

ISBN	TITLE
9788194914129	1984
9789390575220	1984 & Animal Farm (2In1)
9789390575572	1984 & Animal Farm (2In1): The International Best-Selling Classics
9789390575848	35 Sonnets
9789390575329	A Clergyman's Daughter
9789390575923	A Study In Scarlet
9789390896097	A Tale Of Two Cities
9789390896837	Abide in Christ
9789390896202	Abraham Lincoln
9789390896912	Absolute Surrender
9789390896608	African American Classic Collection
9789390575305	Aldous Huxley: The Collected Works
9789390896141	An Autobiography of M. K. Gandhi
9789390575886	Animal Farm
9789390575619	Animal Farm & The Great Gatsby (2In1)
9789390575626	Animal Farm & We
9789390896158	Anna Karenina
9789390575534	Antic Hay
9789390896165	Antony & Cleopatra
9789390896172	As I Lay Dying
9789390896226	As You like it
9789390575671	At Your Command
9789390575350	Awakened Imagination
9789390575114	Be What You Wish
9789390896233	Believe In yourself
9789390896998	Best of Charles Darwin: The Origin of Species & Autobiography
9789390896684	Best Of Horror : Dracula And Frankenstein
9789390575503	Best Of Mark Twain (The Adventures of Tom Sawyer AND The Adventures of Huckleberry Finn)
9789390896769	Black History Collection
9789390575756	Brave New World, Animal Farm & 1984 (3in1)

9789390896240	Brother Karamzov
9789390575053	Bulleh Shah Poetry
9789390575725	Burmese Days
9789390896257	Bushido
9789390896066	Can't Hurt Me
9788194914112	Chanakya Neeti: With The Complete Sutras
9789390896042	Crime and Punishment
9789390575527	Crome Yellow
9789390575046	Down and Out in Paris and London
9789390896844	Dracula
9789390575442	Emersons Essays: The Complete First & Second Series (Self-Reliance & Other Essays)
9789390575749	Emma
9789390575817	Essential Tozer Collection - The Pursuit of God & The Purpose of Man
9789390896578	Fascism What It Is and How to Fight It
9789390575688	Feeling is the Secret
9789390575190	Five Lessons
9789390575954	Frankenstein
9789390575237	Franz Kafka: Collected Works
9789390575282	Franz Kafka: Short Stories
9789390575060	George Orwell Collected Works
9789390575077	George Orwell Essays
9789390575213	George Orwell Poems
9788194914150	Greatest Poetry Ever Written Vol 1
9788194914143	Greatest Poetry Ever Written Vol 1
9789390896301	Gulliver's Travel
9789390575961	Gunaho Ka Devta
9789390575893	H. P. Lovecraft Selected Stories Vol 1
9789390575978	H. P. Lovecraft Selected Stories Vol 2
9789390896059	Hamlet
9789390575022	His Last Bow: Some Reminiscences of Sherlock Holmes
9789390896134	History of Western Philosophy
9789390575121	Homage To Catalonia

9789390896219	How to develop self-confidence and Improve public Speaking
9789390896295	How to enjoy your life and your Job
9789390575633	How to own your own mind
9789390896318	How to read Human Nature
9789390896325	How to sell your way through the life
9789390896370	How to use the laws of mind
9789390896387	How to use the power of prayer
9789390896028	How to win friends & Influence People
9788194824176	How To Win Friends and Influence People
9789390896103	Humility The Beauty of Holiness
9789390896653	Imperialism the Highest Stage of Capitalism
9789390575084	In Our Time
9789390575169	In Our Time & Three Stories and Ten poems
9789390575145	James Allen: The Collected Works
9789390896189	Jesus Himself
9789390575480	Jo's Boys
9789390896394	Julius Caesar
9789390575404	Keep the Aspidistra Flying
9789390896400	Kidnapped
9789390896424	King Lear
9789390575824	Lady Susan
9789390896455	Law of Success
9789390896264	Lincoln The Unknown
9789390575565	Little Men
9789390575640	Little Women
9788194914174	Lost Horizon
9789390896462	Macbeth
9789390896929	Man Eaters of Kumaon
9789390896523	Man The Dwelling Place of God
9789390896349	Man The Dwelling Place of God
9789390575909	Mansfield Park
9788194914136	Manto Ki 25 Sarvshreshth Kahaniya
9789390896509	Marxism, Anarchism, Communism
9789390575664	Mathematical Principles of Natural Philosophy

9788194914198	Meditations
9789390575800	Mein Kampf
9789390575794	Memory How To Develop, Train, And Use It
9789390896486	Mind Power
9789390896585	Money
9789390575039	Mortal Coils
9789390575770	My Life and Work
9789390896035	Narrative of the Life of Frederick Douglass
9789390575152	Neville Goddard: The Collected Works
9789390575985	Northanger Abbey
9789390896530	Notes From Underground
9789390896547	Oliver Twist
9789390575459	On War
9789390575541	One, None and a Hundred Thousand
9789390896554	Othelo
9789390575435	Out Of This World
9789390575015	Persuasion
9789390575510	Prayer The Art Of Believing
9789390575091	Pride and Prejudice
9789390896561	Psychic Perception
9789390575381	Rabindranath Tagore - 5 Best Short Stories Vol 2
9789390575367	Rabindranath Tagore - Short Stories (Masters Collections Including The Childs Return)
9789390575374	Rabindranath Tagore 5 Best Short Stories Vol 1 (Including The Childs Return
9789390896622	Romeo & Juliet
9789390896127	Sanatana Dharma
9789390575596	Seedtime & Harvest
9789390896639	Selected Stories of Guy De Maupassant
9789390575206	Self-Reliance & Other Essays
9789390575176	Sense and Sensibility
9789390575299	Shyamchi Aai
9789390896738	Socialism Utopian and Scientific
9789390896646	Success Through a Positive Mental Attitude
9789390575428	The Adventures of Huckleberry Finn

9789390575183	The Adventures of Sherlock Holmes
9789390575343	The Adventures of Tom Sawyer
9789390896691	The Alchemy Of Happiness
9789390575862	The Art Of Public Speaking
9789390896288	The Autobiography Of Charles Darwin
9788194914181	The Best of Franz Kafka: The Metamorphosis & The Trial
9789390575008	The Call Of Cthulhu and Other Weird Tales
9789390575107	The Case-Book of Sherlock Holmes
9789390896110	The Castle Of Otranto
9789390896745	The Communist Manifesto
9789390575589	The Complete Fiction of H. P. Lovecraft
9789390575497	The Complete Works of Florence Scovel Shinn
9789390896820	The Conquest of Breard
9789390896813	The Diary of a Young Girl
9789390896332	The Diary of a Young Girl The Definitive Edition of the Worlds Most Famous Diary
9789390575701	The Great Gatsby, Animal Farm & 1984 (3In1)
9789390575312	The Greatest Works Of George Orwell (5 Books) Including 1984 & Non-Fiction
9789390575992	The Hound of Baskervilles
9789390896707	The Idiot
9789390896714	The Invisible Man
9789390575657	The Knowledge of the holy
9789390575558	The Law & the Promise
9789390896721	The Law Of Attraction
9789390896776	The Leader in you
9789390896363	The Life of Christ
9789390896196	The Man-Eating Leopard of Rudraprayag
9789390896783	The Master Key to Riches
9789390575268	The Memoirs Of Sherlock Holmes
9789390896479	The Midsummer Night's Dream
9789390575466	The Mill On The Floss
9789390896790	The Miracles of your mind
9789390896660	The Mutual Aid A Factor in Evolution
9789390896448	The Origin of Species

9789390896905	The Peter Kropotkin Anthology The Conquest of Bread & Mutual Aid A Factor of Evolution
9789390896806	The Picture of Dorian Gray
9789390896271	The Picture of Dorian Gray
9789390575275	The Power Of Awareness
9789390896356	The Power of Concentration
9788194824169	The Power of Positive Thinking
9789390575411	The Power of the Spoken Word
9788194914105	The Power Of Your Subconscious Mind
9789390896899	The Power of Your Subconscious Mind
9789390896417	The Principles of Communism
9789390575787	The Psychology Of Mans Possible Evolution
9789390896615	The Psychology of Salesmanship
9789390575732	The Pursuit of God
9789390575398	The Pursuit of Happiness
9789390896851	The Quick and Easy Way to effective Speaking
9789390575947	The Return Of Sherlock Holmes
9789390575138	The Road To Wigan Pier
9789390896981	The Root of the Righteous
9789390575855	The Science Of Being Well
9788194914167	The Science Of Getting Rich, The Science Of Being Great & The Science Of Being Well (3In1)
9789390896011	The Screwtape Letters
9789390896073	The Screwtape Letters
9789390575336	The Secret Door to Success
9789390575695	The Secret Of Imagining
9789390896868	The Secret Of Success
9789390896431	The Seven Last Words
9789390575930	The Sign of the Four
9789390896004	The Sonnets
9789390896516	The Souls of Black Folk
9789390896875	The Sound and The Fury
9789390575244	The State and Revolution
9789390896882	The Story of My Life
9789390896936	The Story Of Oriental Philosophy

9789390896752	The Strange Case of Dr. Jekyll and Mr. Hyde
9789390896943	The Tempest
9789390575916	The Valley Of Fear
9789390575879	The Wind in the willows
9789390896080	The Wind in the willows
9789390575763	Their eyes were watching gofd
9789390575831	Three Stories
9789390896950	Twelfth Night
9789390896592	Twelve Years a Slave
9789390896677	Up from Slavery
9789390896974	Value Price and Profit
9789390896967	Wake Up and Live
9789390896493	With Christ in the School of Prayer
9789390575602	Your Faith is Your Fortune
9789390575473	Your Infinite Power To Be Rich
9789390575251	Your Word is Your Wand
9789390575718	Youth
9789391316099	A Christmas Carol
9789391316105	A Doll's House
9789391316501	A Passage to India
9789391316709	A Portrait of the Artist as a Young Man
9789391316112	A Tale of Two Cities
9789391316747	A Tear and a Smile
9789391316167	Agnes Gray
9789391316174	Alice's Adventures in Wonderland
9789391316136	Anandamath
9789391316181	Anne Of Green Gables
9789391316754	Anthem
9789391316198	Around The World in 80 Days
9789391316013	As A Man Thinketh
9789391316242	Autobiography of a Yogi
9789391316266	Beyond Good and Evil
9789391316761	Bleak House
9789391316778	Chitra, a Play in One Act
9789391316310	David Copperfield

9789391316075	Demian
9789391316785	Dubliners
9789391316051	Favourite Tales from the Arabian Nights
9789391316235	Gitanjali
9789391316068	Gravity
9789391316150	Great Speeches of Abraham Lincoln
9789391316662	Guerilla Warfare
9789391316839	Kim
9789391316822	Mother
9789391316211	My Childhood
9789391316846	Nationalism
9789391316327	Oliver Twist
9789391316853	Pygmalion
9789391316334	Relativity: The Special and the General Theory
9789391316389	Scientific Healing Affirmation
9789391316341	Sons and Lovers
9789391316587	Tales from India
9789391316372	Tess of The D'Urbervilles
9789391316396	The Awakening and Selected Stories
9789391316402	The Bhagvad Gita
9789391316303	The Book of Enoch
9789391316228	The Canterville Ghost
9789391316907	The Dynamic Laws of Prosperity
9789391316006	The Great Gatsby
9789391316860	The Hungry Stones and Other Stories
9789391316433	The Idiot
9789391316440	The Importance of Being Earnest
9789391316297	The Light of Asia
9789391316914	The Madman His Parables and Poems
9789391316457	The Odyssey
9789391316921	The Picture of Dorian Gray
9789391316464	The Prince
9789391316938	The Prophet
9789391316945	The Republic
9789391316518	The Scarlet Letter

9789391316143	The Seven Laws of Teaching
9789391316525	The Story of My Experiments with Truth
9789391316532	The Tales of the Mother Goose
9789391316549	The Thirty Nine Steps
9789391316594	The Time Machine
9789391316600	The Turn of the Screw
9789391316983	The Upanishads
9789391316617	The Yellow Wallpaper
9789391316426	The Yoga Sutras of Patanjali
9789391316990	Ulysses
9789391316624	Utopia
9789391316679	Vanity Fair
9789391316020	What Is To Be Done
9789391316686	Within A Budding Grove
9789391316693	Women in Love